THE POWER
OF PRAYER

Other Thomas Nelson books by Herbert Lockyer:

The Holy Spirit of God
The Keeping Power of God

THE POWER OF PRAYER

Herbert Lockyer

THOMAS NELSON PUBLISHERS

Nashville

Published in Nashville, Tennessee, by Thomas Nelson, Inc., Publishers and distributed in Canada by Lawson Falle, Ltd., Cambridge, Ontario.

Printed in the United States of America.

Unless otherwise indicated, Scripture quotations in this book are from the King James Version of the Bible.

Scripture quotations marked RSV are from the Revised Standard Version of the Bible, copyrighted 1946, 1952, © 1971, 1973.

Although much of the material in this volume originally appeared in Herbert Lockyer's *How I Can Make Prayer More Effective,* the current edition contains new material and has undergone considerable updating and revision—The Publisher.

Library of Congress Cataloging in Publication Data

Lockyer, Herbert.
    Power of prayer.

    1. Prayer. I. Title.
BV210.2.L57   248.3'2   82-3617
ISBN 0-8407-5797-2   AACR2

A Commendation

The following excerpt was taken from a letter by Dr. Thomas A. Carruth, former Field Secretary, *World Wide Prayer Life Movement*.

"In my work as Field Secretary, it has been my privilege to read and examine many excellent books on the subject of Prayer. This unique volume by Dr. Herbert Lockyer is the only book I have ever studied that teaches in a clear, comprehensive way the Christian biblical concept of the place of the Father, the Son, and the Holy Spirit in prayer. This volume might have accurately been entitled, *How I Can Make Prayer More Christian*. There is much prayer that is non-Christian. This book blazes the trail for the Christian who dares to be intellectually honest and face the *total* challenge of the *total gospel* as it is recorded in the Holy Bible. . . . Dr. Lockyer has honored the Christian concept of joy and has kept faith with the Word in giving us this splendid volume."

Contents

Preface

When the publishers invited me to take the time to write a book on prayer, my response was somewhat diffident. Although I've been a Christian for over seventy-five years, I realized the need to tarry longer in the school of prayer before writing about such a holy exercise. The more the proposition was prayerfully considered, however, the more I saw the need to prepare a book calculated to help average Christians.

In these pages I have made no effort to prove the reality of prayer. In this I have heeded the example of the Bible, where prayer's reality is presented as fact and proven by powerful examples. As William Evans once expressed it, "Prayer does not need proof; it needs practice."

Without doubt, prayer is the greatest art in the world, an art that can be learned. If it is a lost art, it is lost only because man has lost his consciousness of God. Dr. Hallesby, whose great book *Prayer* is widely known, wrote:

Prayer is a fine, delicate instrument. To use it right is a great art, a holy art. There is perhaps no greater art than the art of prayer. The other fine arts require a great deal of native ability, much knowledge, and a great deal of money to cover the cost of a long and expensive period of training. Fortunately, such is not the case with the art of prayer. It requires neither great native ability, nor much knowledge, nor money. The least gifted, the uneducated and the poor can cultivate the holy art of prayer. However, certain requirements must also be met, if the art of prayer is to be acquired. In the main, they are two: practice and perseverance.

The conspicuous weakness afflicting present-day Christianity is the lack of Christians praying effectively. Most of us must confess that our Christian life is anemic and powerless because we have not learned the art and discipline of prayer. "The disparity between the prayer-privilege as seen in God's Word, and the prayer-practice as seen in daily life," as Norman Harrison has said, should be a matter of concern to those who desire a Spirit-inspired witness. The difference in spiritual vitality among Christians can be traced to their conception of prayer. The Christian who does not pray is not, and cannot be, a Christian after the New Testament order. And the Christian who does not pray habitually has a hope built on a rotting foundation.

The holiest and most fruitful witnesses for Christ are those who make much of prayer. The greatest preachers of the gospel and missionaries of the Cross are those who come most often and linger longest at the mercy seat of prayer. The saints of the Bible had a unique sense of the presence of God. To them heaven was not far from earth. They treated prayer as an attitude of life, not a series of isolated acts. They viewed prayer as a necessity and, as William E. Gladstone aptly stated, "the highest expression of the human intellect." They believed prayer could bend the arm of God.

It is never easy to pray! It may seem easy, yet nothing is

more difficult. Prayer was once described as "the strangest adventure in human life." It is possible to mouth a written prayer without spiritual, mental, and physical effort; but to pray in the Spirit, to cry out from the heart to heaven, involves pain, planning, and perseverance.

The purpose, then, in this study of the nature of prayer is to explain the simplicity and effectiveness of heart communication with God. The Westminster Shorter Catechism beautifully and clearly expresses the full idea of prayer in these words.

> Prayer is
> an offering up of our desires
> unto God,
> for things agreeable to His will
> in the name of Christ,
> with confession of our sins
> and thankful acknowledgment of our mercies.

The Scottish poet Robert Burns wrote of prayer as "a correspondence fixed with heaven." It is because of this great freedom to establish contact between earth and heaven that "men ought always to pray, and not faint [lose heart]" (Luke 18:1). No matter where we may be on the earth, the ladder of prayer reaching up to heaven stands ready for profitable use. Francis Thompson, in his poem *The Kingdom of God,* has this verse.

> *But when so sad thou canst not sadder*
> *Cry;—and upon thy so sore loss*
> *Shall shine the traffic of Jacob's Ladder*
> *Pitched between Heaven and Charing Cross.*

It is fitting to mention that the substance of this book appeared in 1953 under the title *How I Can Make Prayer More Effective*. This edition, though, has now been revised, expanded, and retitled.*

I believe my labor on this book will not have been in vain if one Christian, with a deep desire to pray, gathers guidance, instruction, and inspiration from the pages that follow. With sincere gratitude I record my indebtedness to the authors of numerous other books, booklets, and articles on prayer, many titles of which are listed in the Suggested Reading section at the end of this book:

Herbert Lockyer
Colorado Springs, Colorado
Autumn, 1981

---

*Sincere gratitude is expressed to Zondervan Publishers for releasing rights to the original book. My large companion volume, *All the Prayers of the Bible,* is published by this renowned firm.

THE POWER
OF PRAYER

1

The Antiquity of Prayer

Prayer is as old as the human race. When God created Adam and Eve, He implanted within them the desire and ability to converse with Him. The sacred narrative in the Book of Genesis reveals that our first parents communed with God. The morning stars were not alone in their songs of praise over a newborn world. Naturally and instinctively, Adam and Eve lifted their voices in homage and praise to their Maker. Even when their disobedience resulted in expulsion from the Garden of Eden, we can imagine that they asked for pardoning mercy at the hand of the Lord. They desired to talk with Him. Is not prayer, in its simplest form, man's innate instinct to talk to God?

Prayer, then, is the oldest and most universal of all religious exercises. Men began in earliest ages to call upon the name of the Lord. Man was born to pray. He has been labeled "a praying animal." Man will pray whether it be to the true God or to an idol of his own creation. Prayer is a dictate of nature, "a constitutional instinct inwrought by the Maker. It is natural and instinctive for man to call upon One greater than himself to aid him in time of need. This is why the most godless cry out to God, when cast into sudden and extreme peril." There is something in the nature of man that leads him to recognize and worship a superior being. Man is a religious being; he will worship.

Prayer is a reality and is supremely natural to man. Of course, some will argue that prayer is a psychological crutch, an unmanly habit of weaklings in the time of need. Others speak of it as superstition. But all men in all ages have prayed. Any disbelief in prayer's reality resides in the opinions, not the impulses, of men. Prayer is a native impulse of the soul. Its custom is as old as human awe and takes countless moods and forms.

The ancient Egyptian used to bully his gods, and the Australian aborigine carried a severed hand to which he would say, "Guide me right or I throw you to the dogs." The Greeks of long ago prayed in short formulas which they believed had magical powers. Plato said, "Every man of sense before beginning any important work will ask help of the gods."

Frederich Heiler, in a study on prayer as a universal element in all early religions, devoted one hundred pages to the prayers and prayer customs of primitive tribes in Africa, Australia, and America. Any examination of the prayer life of pagan tribes reveals a special reverence and awe in the worshippers as they approach the unseen spirit whose dwelling place is high above men and whose attributes are not like those of mortals. As a rule, the prayers of primitives are on a low plane and, if offered by non-Christians, are said in the outer court of the temple, so to speak. They do not have the boldness to approach the holy of holies. Usually, their prayers are for temporal blessings and success. Good crops, rain, healing, peace—these represent the bulk of heathen cries.

Samuel Zwemer, in his volume *Taking Hold of God*,

proves strikingly that there is no tribe or people—no matter how degraded or ignorant of even the beginnings of civilization—that does not pray. Zwemer writes, "Men began to pray and continued to pray because the necessity of their moral nature bade them commune with the unseen." Somehow man feels that he belongs to two worlds, and that prayer is the ladder by which he can climb from the one world to the other.

Today, Moslems prostrate themselves on a rug; Tibetan Buddhists write their supplications on tiny flags and stick them in a mound for the wind to carry away; Roman Catholics finger their rosaries; Quakers sit together in silence. From every corner of the world, at every hour of the day and night, to one god or another, the prayers or meditations of religious beings rise. In the majority of cases, unbiblical prayers are never directly and literally answered, yet men pray on.

Prayer, then, is bound up with the basic beliefs of life. Man, as a religious being, recognizes that prayer is the breath of life, the most divine exercise his heart can engage in. As a created being, man cries out for his Creator. "Thou hast made us for Thyself, and our hearts are restless till they find their rest in Thee," said Saint Augustine. Prayer is the answer to the soul's clamant hunger for God. It is the evidence of an unseen, divine power outside ourselves.

Succeeding chapters will demonstrate that prayer is a working force in Christian experience, that Christians pray, and persist in prayer, because of prayer's effectiveness. The saints of all ages have prayed, not out of sentiment or because prayer was simply an instinct. They have proven that prayer is not a presumption, but rather a worker of miracles in human lives. "Whosoever rises from his prayer a better man," said George Meredith, "that man's prayer is answered." This force of prayer makes saints. As E. M. Bounds expressed it: "Holy characters are formed by the power of real praying. The more of true saints, the more of praying; the more of praying, the more of true saints."

We do not bow down to idols of stone and wood, who may have ears, but hear not. We have the full attention of God, who loves to hear His children pray and can be approached directly through Christ, by the Spirit. He is ever ready to answer Spirit-inspired prayers. But before He answers, we must speak.

2

The Nature of Prayer

What, exactly, is prayer? While it is the most universal and the most intense expression of God-given instincts, yet it is of "all the acts and states of the soul the most difficult to define," wrote Samuel Zwemer. "It escapes definition and is broader, higher, deeper than all human language."

I once heard a gifted Bible expositor, the author of a helpful book on prayer, affirm that prayer is asking, nothing more or less than asking. But is this so? Certainly, asking is an integral part of prayer, for the root idea of "to pray" is "to ask." But surely asking is only one aspect, although a vital and essential part, of the soul's approach to God.

The meaning of Old Testament Hebrew words for prayer is akin to "intercession" or "intervention," with a root meaning of "to judge" or "to entreat." In the New Testament, we find the general term of prayer is *proseuche,* which is a compound word—*pros,* which suggests direction towards, and *euche,* which stands for the simple prayer or vow.

Another word used by the New Testament writers was *deomai,* to ask or beg for, from the root *deo,* to want or need. Still another term is *erotao,* to ask or interrogate, a term employed by Christ in John 14:17. Other words are

19

aiteo, asking, and *enteuxis,* intercession (1 Tim. 2:1), given as prayers in 1 Timothy 4:5. A particularly interesting verse is 1 Timothy 2:1 in which Paul used four different words related to prayer: "I exhort therefore, that, first of all, supplications, prayers, intercessions, and giving of thanks, be made for men." Here we have *deesis* (from *deoamai*), the need and asking side of prayer; *proseuche,* expressing prayer in its general aspect; *enteuxis,* meeting with God; *eucharistia,* from which we have "eucharist," a word meaning thanksgiving. The Latin word for prayer is *precaria* (from which "precarious" comes) and implies something to be obtained by begging or entreaty.

When the disciples, seeing Jesus at prayer, presented their request, "Lord, teach us to pray," He did not reply, "Prayer is simply asking God for what you want." He gave them the model prayer which we call "The Lord's Prayer," in which asking God for what we want is but a minor part. Two thirds of The Lord's Prayer are devoted to worship, adoration, and praise.

It would seem that Jesus condemned excessive asking, since he reminded His disciples that their heavenly Father already knew of their (His creatures') needs. If this is true (it is certainly), then why should we devote so much breath to begging God for those things He knows we have need of? The advice of a sixteenth-century mystic is still relevant: "Prayer is to ask not what we wish of God, but what God wishes of us."

Prayer is many-sided, and there are many ways to label and explain the aspects of prayer. It is spoken of in Scripture as request, incense, intercession, entreaty, complaint, meditation, supplication, waiting, and more. According to the Franciscan pattern, there are eight steps in prayer:

recollection, contrition, devotion, reading, meditation, thanksgiving, oblation or consecration, and petition. The commentator Matthew Henry listed these five parts of prayer: adoration, confession, petition, thanksgiving, and intercession.

Norman Harrison observed: "Prayer is not of an unvarying uniformity in its expression, but rather falls naturally into different phases, or parts, according to the prevailing purpose in view. Our approach to God the Father calls for adoration and worship. Our use of 'the name' leads on to petition and intercession. And the needful accompaniments of prayer call for confession and thanksgiving." Truly, there are many facets to the diamond of prayer.

Prayer, first and foremost, is an act of homage from the creature to the Creator, the highest expression of our allegiance to Him; hence a precious privilege and a binding duty. No matter what phase of prayer we may think of, the very act implies the existence of a Person, One greater than ourselves. We cannot seek help from a wall or an elusive influence. If there is no personal God, then prayer is empty and valueless.

Prayer, then, is not to be merely regarded as a means of getting what we want from God. It is the method by which we give unto the Lord the glory due His name. It involves the highest exercise of adoration of which the human spirit is capable.

There is also devout meditation, or the listening side of prayer (Ps. 46:10). Longfellow must have had this aspect of prayer in mind when he wrote these expressive lines.

Let us, then, labour for an inward stillness—
That perfect silence, where the lips and heart
Are still, and we no longer entertain

Our own imperfect thoughts and vain opinions.
But God alone speaks in us, and we wait,
In singleness of heart, that we may know
His will; and, in the silence of our spirits,
That we may do His will, and do that only.

It will be profitable to examine how various writers have described the nature of prayer. James Montgomery, in his great prayer hymn, revealed a dozen aspects in six stanzas. Prayer to the hymnist was "a sincere desire—often inaudible, a hidden fire, a sigh, a tear, an upward glance to God, the simple lisp of a child, the cry of the prodigal, the breath of the soul, the invigorating mountain air, the watchword at death, the key to heaven, the pathway of Christ."

Other authors have offered these comments on prayer:

Prayer is "the passage from spiritual thirst to spiritual refreshing."

"If prayer is anything, it is everything; if it is truth, it is the greatest truth."

"Prayer is a dialogue, not a monologue; it is a vision as well as a voice; it is a revelation as well as a supplication."

"Prayer is not a mere venture and a voice of mine, but a vision and a voice divine."

John Bunyan said, "Prayer is a sincere, sensible journey out of the soul to God, through Christ, and in the strength and assistance of the Holy Spirit, for such things as God has promised."

Prayer is the "highest exercise of the affections, the will, the memory, the imagination, and the conscience." "Daily prayer is the gymnasium of the soul."

Isaiah, the Old Testament prophet, wrote a definition of prayer surpassing all others in boldness, simplicity, and psychological accuracy: "There is none that calleth upon

thy name, that stirreth up himself to take hold of thee..."
(64:7). The literal Hebrew, said Samuel Zwemer, implies
that prayer means to rouse oneself out of sleep and seize
hold of Jehovah. It implies the pathos of one who is deadly
earnest, the arms, the hands, the very fingers of the soul
reaching out to lay hold of God; prayer is man's personal,
spiritual appropriation of Deity.

E. M. Bounds described the nature of prayer in these
weighty words: "Prayer life has its own laws, as all the rest
of life has. The fundamental law in prayer is this: Prayer is
given and ordained for the purpose of glorifying God.
Prayer is the appointed way of giving Jesus an opportunity
to exercise His supernatural powers of salvation. And in so
doing He desires to make use of us."

Is this our conception of prayer? Having understood
prayer's true nature, are we proving that it is the God-given
way by which our lean souls can be restored to spiritual
health and vigor? Are we proving that all the emotions of
the soul can be exercised in the right way through the
employment of the lost art of secret prayer? If not, may it be
so—and soon!

3

The Philosophy of Prayer

Closely associated with the nature of personal communion with God is a philosophy we must master if we are to know how to pray effectually. Prayer is well-nigh impossible without a primary conviction, namely, that there is a living, personal, intelligent God to whom we pray and with whom man can freely communicate. Accepting such a premise, the question "Why pray?" becomes, rather, "Why not pray?" Belief in God makes prayer a self-justifying achievement.

The quintessence of the philosophy of prayer is asking God in faith for what we need or, rather, for what He wants us to have. The Deist argues that God is too transcendent, too high above man, to be expected to listen to man's prayers. But the Bible affirms that He is not too remote or man too insignificant for prayer to be a vital transaction between God and man. At the heart of prayer there is a lively sense of God's unremitting care for His people. Augustine cried, "O Thou God omnipotent, who carest for every one of us as if Thou carest for him alone; and so for all as if all were one!"

God is likewise omniscient. He sees all and each in all. We appear to be lost in a crowd, but we are not so to God. The psalmist declared that God knows the stars by name

(147:4). The Lord Jesus said that He knows His own by name (John 10:3). Thus prayer becomes real to us as we experience in a personal way through faith that God cares for each one of us.

How real God was to the saints of old! They had no doubt as to the true import of prayer. Think of Psalm 31, where the writer goes to God in the confidence that He is his strong rock and his fortress (vv. 2,3). Men had forgotten the psalmist, and he distrusted them. But triumphantly he declared, "I trusted in thee, O LORD," and then he reveals his assurance in retrospection (vv. 7,8), committal (v. 5), confidence in God's justice (vv. 17,18), prayer (vv. 1,2), praise (vv. 19,20), and testimony (v. 23).

Sound, normal, effective prayer can only be ours as we respect and obey God's laws which govern prayer. If we disregard these laws, or act contrary to the idea and essence of prayer, how can we pray correctly? Four things are superlatively essential, according to William W. Horner: "righteous living, faith in God, the guidance of the Holy Spirit, and the will of God." We all possess the "noble capacity for prayer," but it only becomes a vital force in our life when we turn to God in perfect simplicity and naturalness, knowing that He knows, loves, and cares.

George Mueller, that mighty man of prayer, who trusted God implicitly for his orphans, has left for us his philosophy of prayer in this unforgettable way.

1. "I seek at the beginning to get my heart into such a state that it has no will of its own in regard to a given matter. Nine-tenths of the trouble with people is just here. Nine-tenths of the difficulties are overcome when our hearts are ready to do the Lord's will, whatever it

may be. When one is truly in this state, it is usually but a little way to the knowledge of what His will is.

2. "Having done this, I do not leave the result to feeling or simple impression. If I do so, I make myself liable to great delusions.

3. "I seek the will of the Spirit of God through, or in connection with, the Word of God. The Spirit and the Word must be combined. If I look to the Spirit alone, without the Word, I lay myself open to great delusions also. If the Holy Spirit guides us at all, He will do it according to the Scriptures and not apart from them.

4. "Next I take into account the providential circumstances. These often plainly indicate God's will in connection with His Word and His Spirit.

5. "I ask God in prayer to reveal His will to me aright.

6. "Thus, through prayer to God, the study of the Word and reflection, I come to a deliberate judgment according to the best of my ability and knowledge, and if my mind is thus at peace and continues so after two or three more petitions, I proceed accordingly."

In his heart-stirring volume, *Quiet Talks on Prayer,* S. D. Gordon discussed what he termed "The Law of Prayer Action." These guidelines will help insure a correct philosophy and practice of prayer.

1. Prayer must be in Jesus' name.
2. Prayer must be by a person in full touch with Jesus, in heart, habit, and life.

3. Prayer must be in harmony with the teaching of the Bible.
4. Prayer must be actual, simple, definite, and confident—"in faith believing."

These sublime lines, humbly received, should stir us to nurture an effective practice of prayer.

> *'Tis not enough to bend the knee,*
> *And words of prayer to say;*
> *The heart must with the lips agree;*
> *Or else we do not pray:*
> *For words, without the heart,*
> *The Lord will never hear;*
> *Nor will he to those lips attend,*
> *Whose prayers are not sincere.*

4

The Privilege of Prayer

Although we often sing about the privilege of carrying everything to God in prayer, we must confess the tendency to take this blessed privilege for granted. Who are we, that we should be able to take God's name upon our lips and tell Him all that is upon our hearts? He is high and holy, the Lord God Almighty; yet we mortals have authority to come before Him at any time, in any place, and commune with Him! We do not have to wait upon any whim or movement of God. The services of a human intermediary are unnecessary. No matter who we are or where we are, by grace we have the right to come immediately into the presence of Him who bids His children ask and receive. Social and other barriers may keep us from conversing with important government leaders or celebrities in our land. But we may approach the King of Kings at any time in any place.

William Wallace Horner reminds us that "among the callings and privileges accorded to God's children, prayer holds the supreme place and is of inestimable value both to the pray-er and to those for whom he prays."

Our common tragedy is the failure to take advantage of such a priceless privilege. We are not victorious in life and fruitful in service because the communication line with heaven is not in constant use. Privileged with daily opportunities of dwelling with the King and appropriating all His wealth of power and wisdom, we yet live as those who delight in penury.

Old Testament saints understood something of the privilege of approaching God. But during those times, God localized His presence in the temple, and the Jew *had* to go there to pray. Under grace, the spirit—not the mere sphere of worship—is all-important (John 4:24). The child of God can draw nigh to Him anywhere. Such is his broad privilege that through Christ he can converse with Him in barn or cathedral. God is no respecter of places. And, as the hymn reminds us, we forfeit much peace of mind, all because we fail to take full advantage of the blessed, exalted privilege of prayer. A full recognition of the privilege of prayer will save us from any irreverence, undue familiarity, or unpreparedness as we enter the presence of God.

Our conception of the privilege of prayer does influence the manner of our approach to God. If one remembers that it is "the King eternal, immortal, invisible, the only wise God" who offers us immediate access into His presence, then we will desire to exercise all due reverence and humility. When the Jews of old came before Him, they bowed their heads and worshipped. The Bible reveals that as the Seraphim wait before Him, they veil their faces and acclaim Him as the thrice-holy Lord, almighty God. This being the case, how dare we be unduly familiar with Him before whom the whole court of heaven bows in submission?

A scriptural understanding of the privilege of prayer likewise will prevent us from treating God as, more or less, an equal—One with whom we can barter and selfishly petition: "Tell you what I'll do, God: let's make a deal. You give me this, and I'll do that." No, such an attitude is an abuse of our privilege; it is a modern manifestation of the primitive sacrifice, an offer to trade incense for luck.

The words *boldness* and *confidence* used in connection with prayer (Eph. 3:12, Heb. 4:16 and 10:19–22), words that signify freedom of speech or liberty to ask anything, sufficiently indicate the inestimable privilege of prayer, but in no way encourage license or flippant familiarity (Ps. 89:7). We need to echo these appealing words of Montgomery.

> *Lord, teach us how to pray aright,*
> *With reverence and with fear;*
> *Though dust and ashes in Thy sight,*
> *We may, we must draw near.*
> *Give deep humility, the sense*
> *Of godly sorrow give;*
> *A strong, desiring confidence,*
> *To hear Thy voice, and live.*

Prayer is heaven's telephone line which is free to all, always available, never out of order. The line, however, must always be used with reverence and godly fear. Prayer is a priceless privilege.

5

The Necessity of Prayer

Prayer is not only an instinct and a privilege, but a divine and human imperative. Jesus reminded His own of the necessity of prayer in the words, "Men ought always to pray" (Luke 18:1). "We will never pray as we should until we see it as a necessity," said Norman Harrison, "indispensable to the life we have undertaken to live." Then this gifted brother went on to state seven outstanding reasons for prayer's necessity:

1. To honor God as our Father (Matt. 7:7–11).
2. To discharge our office as priests (1 Pet. 2:5,9).
3. To avail ourselves of our new privilege as believers (John 16:24).
4. To fulfill our obligation to fellow-believers (Eph. 6:18).
5. To seek and to save the souls of men (1 Tim. 2:4).
6. To outwit and overcome the powers of evil (Eph. 6:11,12 and 1 Pet. 5:8,9).
7. To grow personally in grace and godliness (1 Tim. 4:7 and 2 Pet. 3:18).

Prayer is as necessary to our spiritual well-being as fresh air is to our physical welfare. Perhaps it was this thought that led James Montgomery to speak of prayer as "the Christian's vital breath, the Christian's native air."

We not only grieve the Lord but injure our own souls when we are "hindering meditation before God" (Job 15:4 RSV). Even when we are not engaged directly in public or family worship, it is necessary to live in unbroken contact with heaven.

While all that is needful and beneficial has been divinely promised, prayer is essential if we are to appropriate these promises. "... 'I will yet for this be inquired of by the house of Israel, to do it for them'..." (Ezek. 36:37).

William Proctor reminds us that "the necessity of prayer is evident from what is recorded of its results in the individual and corporate life of the Early Church, as compared with those in the Modern Church.... We have better organization, sounder scholarship, and more eloquent preaching, but we have less fervent, individual prayer—and earnest, united intercession." The Book of Acts, so full of prayer, proves this point. To the apostles there could not be any power for holy service apart from communion with God.

Christ ever recognized His need of prayer. What utter dependence upon the Father He manifested! To Him it was no pleasant, hurried pastime, but an agony of desire. Strong crying and tears accompanied His supplications. E. M. Bounds once wrote: "Prayer is not a little habit pinned on to us while we are tied to our mother's apron-strings, neither is it a little decent quarter-of-a-minute's grace said over an hour's dinner, but it is a most serious work of our most serious years...."

How does John Bunyan's Christian, walking through the valley of the shadow of death on that narrow pathway between the quagmire and the pit, with horrible creeping things around his feet and foul fiends hissing in his ears, meet his peril? Christian casts aside his sword and takes to himself the weapon of prayer. In this picture of the soul fighting foes without and fears within, there is a forceful lesson for our hearts to learn. As good soldiers of Jesus Christ, prayer is our most necessary and effective weapon against the world, the flesh, and the devil.

Prayer, as a spiritual weapon, acts in a twofold way.

1. *It is a weapon of defense.* We can claim protection for the body against weakness, disease, or accident (James 5:13–16); for the mind against deceit, delusion, and discouragement (Mark 1:32–39); for the spirit against bad moods, jealousy, and hardness (Ps. 51:10); for the will against paralyzing fear or crippling indecision (Ps. 27). Defense for any phase of life can be claimed by prayer. Daniel, threatened with death because of a demand to recall a dream of the king and to reveal its content, solved a humanly impossible problem with prayer (Dan. 2:14–23). He wanted to know God's plans; praying, he received an answer (Dan. 9).

2. *It is a weapon of offense.* Often secret prayer is related to public action. Waiting upon and for God, we get our plan of attack. Prayer is vision, unfolding God's purpose for life and service. Prayer is also the secret of inspiration. Strength, courage, and endurance become ours to fullfill the divine purpose as we pray. It will benefit you to meditate upon some of the great "fighting" prayers of the Bible, those of Asa (2 Chr. 14:11), Jehoshaphat (2 Chr. 20:6–13), Hezekiah (Is. 37:14–20), and Nehemiah (Neh. 4:9).

"Prayer and helplessness are inseparable," E. M. Bounds has said. Man's desire to approach God is in effect an admittance of his inability to do anything unless divine aid is forthcoming. The more conscious we are of our utter inability and weakness, the greater the intensity of our prayers. Looking into the face of God, our own vaunted wisdom and fancied strength quickly disappear. Someone has said, "Only he who is helpless can truly pray."

Too many of us have a weak prayer life simply because we are puffed up with our own self-knowledge, self-sufficiency, self-ability. We know it all, can do it all, so why pray? But apart from Christ, we are nothing, and can do nothing (Phil. 4:13). Hartley Coleridge put it well:

> *Pray, if thou canst, with hope; but ever pray*
> *Though hope be weak, or sick with long delay;*
> *Be not afraid to pray; to pray is right,*
> *Pray in the darkness, if there is no light.*

6

The Foundation of Prayer

While reaching God is the chief objective in prayer, prayer
is futile unless we come to Him as He directs. And because
of the importance of prayer, God tells us how He functions
as the Hearer and the Answerer of prayer. All within the
blessed Trinity are involved: (1) God the Father promises to
heed the cry of His own; (2) God the Son, by His sacrificial
death, provided an access into the holiest of all, and through
His resurrection and ascension has taken His place as our
great High Priest, to respond to those prayers offered in His
name; and (3) God the Spirit prompts true prayer. We do not
know how to pray properly but He helps us overcome this
infirmity.

Thus the triune God is associated with our petitions,
which are ever effective when we come to God, through
Christ, by the Spirit.

Chief among the foundational principles of prayer is the
right use of the name of Christ. If prayer is to be acceptable
it must be offered in His name (John 14:13,14 and 15:16). If
we use the name of a friend instead of our own, we deny
ourselves and identify with the friend's name. Such an
action certainly links two persons together.

Using the name of Christ does not mean that we lightly

and mechanically append it to our prayers, as we tie a label to a parcel. Asking in Christ's name is more than a customary formula; it involves correspondence with His will and harmony with His wishes (Acts 19:13–16).

There is a "Dead Prayer Office," just as there is a "Dead Letter Office." Many of our prayers lose their way because they are wrongly addressed. Jesus said, "No man cometh unto the Father, *but by me*" (John 14:6, italics added). Therefore, no matter how religious a person may appear to be, if he denies the mediation and advocacy of Christ and approaches God in a way of his own choosing, his prayers are futile. Apart from Christ we are spiritually bankrupt, having nothing to our credit. Our bountiful Father accepts only those checks drawn and presented in the only name honored in heaven's bank—the peerless name of Jesus.

Another clear-cut direction for acceptable prayer is that it must be in full accord with the will of God (1 John 5:14,15). Too often our prayers project our own will and wishes. Jesus prayed, "Not *my* will, but thine be done." There are prayers which remain unanswered—those stained with petulant self-will.

Another key to prayer response is the recognition of the Holy Spirit as "the Guide of prayer and the Guarantor of its success." The clear revelation in the New Testament of how prayer works stresses the part the Holy Spirit plays in our intercession (Rom. 8:26, Eph. 2:18, and Jude 20).

Faith is the indispensable condition for answered prayer: "If ye have faith, and doubt not" (Matt. 21:21). Faith is the means of communication with the invisible God, and it is essential to the offering and answering of prayer (Heb. 11:6 and James 1:6,7). "Many of our prayers fail to enter heaven," says William Proctor, "for the same reason that a whole generation of Israelites failed to enter Canaan, 'because of unbelief' (Heb. 3:18,19, cf. Matt. 17:19–21).''

There is a vital connection between prayer and faith. To quote Proctor again:

> Faith is prayer in the heart, and prayer is faith on the lips. . . . Prayer is the key to all the treasures of Divine Grace, it opens all the doors and gives access to all the stores; but faith is the hand that uses the key.

No matter how great the petition presented, "Faith laughs at impossibility, and cries, 'It shall be done.'"

At the foundation of all prayer must be that absolute reliance upon the promises of God (2 Sam. 7:28,29). What God has promised, He is able to perform; and we prayerfully must appropriate His promises. The precious promises of God are both our warrant for praying and our security for receiving. We have no authority to ask for anything beyond the all-embracing scope of great promises that cover all of our needs for body, soul, and spirit.

No saint need have any doubt about the fulfillment of any divine promise, since a divine promise rests upon three great and glorious facts.

1. The truthfulness of God. He cannot deny Himself. He is not a man that He should lie. He must be true to His own character (Num. 23:19 and Heb. 6:18).
2. The love of God. Earthly love can forget a promise, but God's perfect love will not permit Him to forget all He has promised to us (Is. 49:15).
3. The power of God. Because He is almighty, He has the ability to perform all He has promised. Not one word can fail (Gen. 18:14 and Luke 1:37).

Another building block of effectual prayer is "a life inwardly right and outwardly upright," to use Norman Harrison's telling phrase. Prayer and purity are partners. "It is as we live that we pray. It is the life that prays." It is not what we try to be when praying, but what we are when not praying that gives power to our prayer life. It is sadly possible to be indifferent regarding the claim of God upon our life, yet to run to Him in every emergency. He becomes only a life raft in a time of crisis. What a mean action! Unless we ask God for forgiveness of our sins so that we may pray with holy hearts and hands, God refuses to hear (Ps. 66:18). Unless we pray without wrath, God is silenced by our injury of a brother (Mark 11:25). Let us therefore heed the advice of C. H. Spurgeon and "prepare our prayers by preparing ourselves" (1 John 3:22). The whole man should be one burning prayer.

D. M. Panton, discussing the basic ingredients of prayer, said:

1. It should be *brief* (Eccl. 5:2). One stone flung hard is better than a handful of loose gravel.
2. It should be *humble* (Luke 18:13), for "pride is Satan's wedge for splitting prayer meetings to pieces."
3. It should be *pointed* (Phil. 4:6). Every prayer should be full of pointed phrases and definite petitions.
4. It should be scriptural (Rom. 12:2 and James 4:3). To pray scripturally is a safe way to pray according to the will of God.
5. It should be offered in *faith* with *gratitude* (James 1:7). Faith and thankfulness are the wings of prayer (1 Thess. 5:18) which lift it readily to the throne.
6. It should be *intense* (Deut. 4:29). Satan can build

walls around us, but no roof overhead; but our lethargy—mere liturgy—can build a ceiling to our prayers.

Finally, we must never forget that Satan is out to block our prayers. He is an obstinate and determined foe and fighter and, when it comes to strategy, has the accumulated wisdom of thousands of years. The praying believer is the target of satanic antagonism and can only be victorious over the wiles of the enemy as he continuously pleads the name and the blood of the Redeemer. Praise be to God, though, in the prayer-conflict, Calvary gives the child of God the advantage! "They overcame him [the devil, the accuser] by the blood of the Lamb" (Rev. 12:11).

7

The Habits of Prayer

Because prayer is both an art and an attitude, there are some aspects of the theme which, while they do not touch the essentials of prayer, yet call for consideration. These will be considered in this chapter and the next. Set forth below are some practical and profitable suggestions from Scripture, as well as from the spiritual experiences of the saints of God through the ages, regarding the habits of prayer.

The Place of Prayer

The place of prayer matters little. The *spirit* is the all-important factor. Scripture is filled with examples of "extraordinary" settings for prayer:

- Jacob found that desert stones can become an altar.
- Jonah prayed in the belly of a fish.
- Peter prayed in a storm-tossed ship.
- Hagar cried to God in the heart of a desert.
- Hezekiah prayed to the Lord on his sick bed.
- David, hiding in his cave, sought the Lord.
- The penitent thief prayed from a cross.

God's ear is open to our cry, whether by the riverside (Acts 16:13), on the seashore (Acts 21:5), on a housetop (Acts 10:9), on a mountain (Luke 6:12), or on a battlefield (1 Sam. 7:9).

The Samaritan woman whom our Lord met at the well was concerned about the place of worship, for to the Jew the temple meant the localization of God's presence. Christ, however, revealed something new concerning prayer and worship: "God is a Spirit: and they who worship him must worship him in spirit and in truth" (John 4:24). Now, through grace, we can converse with God anywhere.

While, of course, environment should be as favorable as possible when we come before God, it is wonderful to know that we can pray inwardly, if not outwardly, in the most unfavorable surroundings. We can learn to shut the door, even amid conditions that would otherwise bring disturbance. As the apostle Paul said, "I will therefore that men pray *every where,* lifting up holy hands without wrath and doubting" (1 Tim 2:8, italics added).

Ordinarily, a believer should have a regular place for prayer. "Enter into thy closet." Many saints have a place made sacred by habitual meetings with God. Bishop Handley Moule loved to pray and meditate as he walked in his garden. It is essential, if at all possible, to have a definite place, as secluded as possible, where we can be free from distraction and interruption and where we can pray audibly, thereby guarding against wandering thoughts. Where there is a will to find "a place where Jesus sheds the oil of gladness on our heads," there will be a way to find such a place.

The Posture in Prayer

No exclusive posture during prayer is prescribed in the Bible. It is certain, though, that God wants us to shun all slovenly habits when we speak to Him. The Bible does associate several postures or gestures with prayer. Here are some examples.

1. *The lifting up of hands* is a customary attitude adopted both in prayer and praise (Ex. 9:33, Ps. 28:2, and 1 Tim. 2:8). For the psalmist the lifting up of hands toward heaven was a synonym for prayer itself (Ps. 141:2). Charles Wesley had this posture in mind when he wrote:

> *Father, I stretch my hands to Thee,*
> *No other hope I know;*
> *If Thou withdraw Thyself from me,*
> *Ah! whither shall I go?*

2. *Sitting* is another prayer posture. In David's prayer of gratitude we find him sitting (2 Sam. 7:18). Some writers believe that this is the least reverent position of the body and should not be taken as a precedent. Possibly, because of his old age, David was obliged to sit. In such matters, every believer should be persuaded fully in his own mind. Personally, the writer has his most blessed hours when "sitting before the Lord."

3. *Standing* was the usual Jewish position during prayer (1 Sam. 1:26, Neh. 9:4, and Mark 11:25). Subjects usually stand in the presence of their sovereign. Hannah, praying for her son; Solomon, blessing the congregation; Jeremiah, offering his intercession—all of

them stood. The Pharisees, the disciples, the publican, all stood as they prayed. In our day, many, because of affliction, are not able to stand. In public prayer, though, it may be fitting to stand. (Preachers, however, should not take too long in praying if the people are called upon to stand. Weary mothers and hard-working men have been on their feet long enough!)

4. *Kneeling* is a reverent attitude adopted by others. Daniel (Dan. 6:10), Stephen (Acts 7:60), Peter (Acts 9:40), and Paul (Eph. 3:14) all knelt, at least at times. In Bible days, ordinarily prayer was offered kneeling or standing, with adoring prostration at the beginning and the end.

5. *Prostration* is another biblical posture. Ezekiel fell on his face as he beheld the glory of the Lord (Ezek. 3:23, 9:8, and 11:13). This was the posture of Christ in Gethsemane. The angels also prostrate themselves before the Lord.

6. *Eyes were usually open* during prayer. The publican "would not so much as lift up his eyes unto heaven." Jesus prayed with open eyes (Mark 6:41, 7:34, and John 17:1). How the custom of closing eyes when praying developed is uncertain. Certainly, closed eyes do shut out much that would distract our attention.

While posture is of minor importance, it is evident that careless habits can void much power in prayer. We must choose the posture best fitted to our own realization of the divine presence and not condemn others who adopt different habits. Ever remember these truth-filled lines:

Tis not to those who stand erect,
Or those who bend the knee,
It is to those who bend the heart
The Lord will gracious be;
It is the posture of the soul
That pleases, or offends;
If it be not in God's sight right,
Naught else can make amends.

The Period for Prayer

The time we give to prayer is governed by desire, need, circumstances, and physical ability. Often we hear the remark, "I have so little time for prayer." Well, because of its necessity, we must *make* time for communion with God. The most active person needs to pray the most. It is as sensible for a jet pilot to say he has no time to take on fuel, as for the Christian to say he has no time for prayer. James Stalker, in his *Imago Christi,* wrote:

Jesus appears to have devoted Himself specially to prayer at times when His life was unusually full of work and excitement.... Many in our day know what this congestion of occupation is: they are swept off their feet with their engagements and can scarcely find time to eat. We make this a reason for not praying; Jesus made it a reason for praying. Is there any doubt about which is the better course?

One cannot prescribe a hard-and-fast rule as to how long another should pray. This is a matter of individual responsibility. The Bible enjoins us to pray always (Eph. 6:18) and to pray without ceasing (1 Thess. 5:17). The saints who have been mightily used by God have been those who made the time for prayer a notable feature of their lives. For example:

- Charles Simeon devoted four hours a day to definite prayer.
- Charles Wesley, the renowned hymnist, gave two hours daily to prayer.
- John Wesley rose at four to pray, deeming this his greatest task.
- Bishop Lancelot Andrews spent five hours daily in prayer and meditation. No wonder his *Private Devotions* is an immortal spiritual classic.
- John Fletcher sometimes prayed all night.
- Martin Luther had to have three hours a day in prayer.
- Bishop Ken was with God before the clock struck three each morning.
- Joseph Alleine rose at four and felt ashamed if he heard tradesmen at work before his morning prayer began.
- John Welch, mighty Scottish preacher, felt a day was lost if he did not spend eight to ten hours in prayer.
- Judson of Burma, strong advocate of prayer, said that time must be given to God. Begin at midnight, then dawn, and during the day half a dozen times, was his advice.

Space fails us to speak of David Brainerd, David Livingstone, Hudson Taylor, Mary Slessor, Praying Hyde, and James Gilmore, as well as a host of others, who cause us to hang our heads in shame when we say we have so little time for prayer.

The Bible makes it clear that we can pray at any time, for

God never sleeps, and His ear is ever open to our cry. If, amid the cares, irksome duties, and responsibilities of life, we want to know the best time for the cultivation of the soul by prayer and meditation, Bible saints offer a variety of answers.

- Daniel, the prime minister, prayed upon his knees three times a day (Dan. 6:10).
- David prayed in the evening, morning, and at noon (Ps. 55:17).
- Paul urged the saints to pray at all times and unceasingly. Paul and Silas prayed and praised at the midnight hour.
- Jesus prayed early in the morning, sometimes at night. He had to pray; it was His life. That is why we read of Him alone in prayer and ever continuing in prayer. What a tense prayer life was the Master's! "Being in agony," He prayed. He arose "a great while before daybreak to pray." No wonder He urged His own "always to pray and not to faint."

Summarizing Bible teaching concerning the time element in prayer, we note these points.

1. *There should be regular periods of prayer.* Busy men like David and Daniel were careful to let nothing interfere with their devotions (Ps. 55:17 and Dan. 6:10). Matthew Hale, late Lord Chief Justice of England, gave this advice: "Be obstinately constant in your devotions at certain set times." Your circumstances will determine the best time for you.

2. *There should be a morning watch.* No matter how

brief a period can be set aside in the morning, the opening of the day is the best time for prayer. In the morning the mind is fresh and relatively free from distractions. With one saint of old, we too should seek the face of God before we see the face of man: "Thy first transaction be with God Himself above; so shall thy business prosper well, and all the day be love."

3. *There should be a noonday upward glance.* At noon, the two hands of the clock point in the same direction—upward. There is no need to pause and assume any prayer posture. No matter where we may be, knowing that the hands of the clock are pointed heavenward, we can pray silently and thank God for His continual goodness. James Montgomery would have us sing,

> *At noon, beneath the Rock*
> *Of Ages rest and pray;*
> *Sweet is the shadow from the heat,*
> *When the sun smites by day.*

4. *There should be an evening sacrifice.* When the day is over, we need to ask pardon for our sins, to express gratitude for God's mercies, and then to seek His protection through the night (Ps. 4:8, 42:8, and 141:2). Quaint George Herbert said, "Who goes to bed and does not pray, maketh two nights of every day."

After an exhausting day at home or work, we may be too physically and mentally tired to spend much time in prayer. Many a weary worker has fallen asleep on his knees. At times after a long, tiring day, there is just enough energy left to speak a few words to our Lord. Make no doubt about it, the pitying Master understands and accepts such a prayer; for it is not the length of a prayer but the spirit of it that counts with Him. Robert Murray McCheyne once wrote, "I ought not to give up the good old habit of praying before going to bed; but guard must be kept against sleep. Planning what things I am to ask is the best remedy."

5. *There should be whispered prayers.* Frank Laubach, in his most unusual book, *Prayer—The Mightiest Force in the World,* speaks of "flash prayers, swift prayers, broadcast prayers, whisper prayers." Nehemiah often made use of ejaculatory or "flash" prayer (Neh. 2:4; 4:4,5; 5:19; 6:9; 6:14; 13:14,22,29,31). ("Ejaculatory" is from a Latin word meaning "swift darts." The term was used in ancient warfare.) The quickest way to counteract the fiery darts, as they unexpectedly reach us, is through fervent darts of prayer. Let us guard, however, against the temptation to devote all of our time for intimate communication with God only to this type of prayer.

We can learn to pray by the clock if we cannot pray by the heartbeat and thereby form a profitable prayer habit. Dr. Laubach exhorts us to "use chunks of idle, wasted time to send up dart prayers. Upon awaking in the morning. In the bath or shower. Dressing. Walking downstairs. Asking grace at table. Leaving the house. Riding or walking to work. Entering the elevator. Between interviews. Preparing for lunch. And a hundred more chunks all day long, until crawling into bed and falling asleep."

The best of us are conscious that we need God every minute, all day long. Therefore, our whole life should become a prayer. Further, because of our constant need we must take time to pray. Edith H. Kenney's lines are apt at this point.

> *There is always a time in the morning's prime,*
> *And the golden noontide fair;*
> *There is always time 'neath the evening chime,*
> *There is always time for prayer.*
> *When your weary feet falter in the path,*
> *Though to pause you do not dare,*
> *Would you find the stress of the day grow less?*
> *There is always time for prayer.*

8

The Habitat of Prayer

Our study now turns to the habitat or place of prayer. Because our prayer life has both corporate and personal aspects, let us briefly consider three biblical modes of prayer.

Read Colossians 1:9-18a Living Bible

United Prayer

It has been said that a man is only half of himself, his friends are the other half of him. How true this is in respect to prayer. There are times when a person can labor on his own; at other times a team is needed. Many of us struggle on with a burden which could have been lifted long ago if only we had asked others to pray with and for us. *Pause*

Think of the way the Word of God exalts the value of united prayer! In Matthew 18:19,20 and Daniel 2:17,18 we find the limit of those gathering for united prayer fixed downward to a small number, only *two or three*. Numbers do not matter to God, so long as those banded together for prayer are in "one accord" (Acts 1:4; 2:1,46; and 4:24). (It is from the Greek word for "accord" that we get our English word "symphony," implying harmony of thought and feeling.)

eg Acts 2:1- They were "all together in one place" when the Holy Spirit came for the 1st time on the day of pentecost.

Unity in prayer greatly helps to banish the spirit of independence and narrowness of personal outlook, and it benefits our spiritual life in general. That is why we should love the prayer meeting of the church, and we mean *prayer* meeting, such as the ones where the church of Jesus Christ was born and grew (Acts 1:4; 2:1,46; 12:12, and 16:13). Such meetings are ever the spiritual thermometer of a church, and unity in prayer means much to the cause of Christ among men. When in a prayer meeting, we should keep praying all through the meeting. We should cultivate a deep consciousness of God's presence, and continue pleading, even when not praying audibly.

Family Prayer

Family prayer goes back to the early days of the Bible, when the head of the household was the priest. Wherever the patriarchs pitched their tents, they erected an altar (Gen. 12:7,8; 13:3,4). In our day, a home where people pause to pray is a God-blessed home. Someone has said that "a home without prayer is like a house without a roof." Is yours a roofless house? Or is your home being blessed like Obededom's because of the ark (2 Sam. 6:11,12)? The hope of America is not in its nuclear devices, but in altars— places where people cry out to God. A family altar in each of the country's millions of homes would make America the mightiest spiritual force the world has ever known.

What about your home? Is it professedly religious yet destitute of a regular time for Bible study, worship, and prayer? Did you once have such an altar, but now it is broken down? Erect it again! Pray and offer praise in your dwelling, and many of your family troubles will cease. An anonymous writer penned these memorable lines nearly four hundred years ago.

Whom God hath made the heads of families
He hath made priests to offer sacrifice;
Daily let part of Holy Writ be read,
Let, as the body, so the soul have bread:
For look how many souls in thy house be
With just as many souls God trusteth thee.

Secret Prayer

While Scripture records instances of public united prayer, it has much to say about secret prayer as well (Matt. 6:6). Our Lord spoke of the place of prayer: "enter into thy closet"; then, He drew attention to the privacy of prayer: "shut thy door." Unfortunately, it is possible to shut the closet door upon the world and yet carry the atmosphere of the world into the closet!

The world will never know, neither will we as individuals, how the secret prayers of others on our behalf have influenced us. The dear saint J. H. Jowett had his closet. It was an upper room in his home where two chairs stood—one always empty—a table, and a Bible. Seated in one chair, Dr. Jowett would converse with his Lord, whom he imagined to be in the other chair. Here he spent hours with his Master, over the Word.

Jesus has taught us to "pray to the Father which is in secret," for alone with God we can bare our souls. What cannot be told to human ears can be poured into His sympathetic ear. Alone with Him we can speak intimately about our unsaved loved ones with the assurances that He who hears will answer. No one knows of our secret prayers, but we see them changing things and persons. Of course, we, too, are changed, for intimate communion such as this results in transformation (Ex. 34:29,30).

Is it not true that the saints of all ages have been men of the closet? They have proven that "solitude is the mother country of the strong." Let's recall some of these spiritual giants:

- Abraham, when great darkness covered him, kept lonely vigil over his sacrifice.
- Moses, at the burning bush in the desert, was alone with God.
- Elijah, on Carmel and in the cave, also experienced the blessedness of being alone with God.
- David Livingstone, on his knees in his Chitambo hut, prayed and died alone.
- The secret place of Jonathan Edwards was on the bank of the Hudson River.
- David Brainerd spoke of his "secret prayer...in the woods."

We must not forget that Jesus also had a sacred garden spot, to which He often retreated to pray in solitude. Judas knew the place, and one of the more despicable aspects of his crime was that he led Christ's enemies to this garden of secret prayer.

Wonderful indeed are the habits and habitat of prayer. Method is of no great consequence, whether we pray in silence like Hannah, or in secret thought like Nehemiah, or aloud like the Syrophoenician woman, or in tears like Magdalene, or in joy like Paul.

Age likewise does not count. The children, like Samuel, can speak to God, or youths like Daniel and his friends, or grown folks like the Centurion, or the aged, like old Simeon.

Position or nationality form no barrier to prayer. Whether black or white, red or yellow, male or female, rich or poor, saved or lost—all can come to God. The one thing to remember is that we cannot pray by proxy. No priest can act on our behalf. Prayer must be a personal, living force in our own life.

Have you forsaken the altar of prayer? Have success, love, business, home, the cares of life crowded prayer out of your days? Perhaps you used to "take time to be holy and speak oft with your Lord." Now you only give Him a passing word—if any at all. Have you become prayerless? If so, just put this book down, get on your knees, and ask God to restore your lost passion for prayer.

9

The Pattern of Prayer

Perfect prayer patterns are scattered throughout the Bible, and observance of their underlying principles and organization is of immense help in framing our own petitions. When Jesus said to His disciples, "After this *manner* pray ye," He was not implying that they were to take His words and repeat them *verbatim*. He was outlining a plan of approach and was referring to the spirit, the general features, of prayer.

While much of the rich and expressive prayer phraseology of Bible saints will unconsciously become part of our prayers (and the strongest prayers are those saturated with Scripture), we must be careful not merely to reiterate the prayer-language of others. Seeking the Spirit's aid in our intercessions, we must cultivate a clear accent of our own. David could not fight in Saul's armor. The sling and the pebble were more natural to the shepherd lad.

Because the wealth of material at our disposal in respect to prayer examples is great and varied, we will only study a few here.

Prayers in the Old Testament

Abraham, the friend of God, was a spiritual giant in the realm of prayer. His prayer of intercession for the cities of the plain is incomparable (Gen. 18:23–33). In another record of Abraham's communion with God, we see how prayer includes listening (Gen. 13:14–18). Too often prayer is a one-sided exercise, and we do all the talking. Here God speaks to His friend. We should note four aspects of "listening," a neglected side of prayer.

1. *It was the place of separation.* "And the Lord said unto Abram *after* that Lot was separated from him" (13:14). Certain company hinders fellowship with God.
2. *It was the place of vision.* "Lift up now thine eyes, and look" (13:14). If too absorbed with daily activities and common tasks, we become blind to eternal realities.
3. *It was the place of promise.* "For all the land which thou seest, to thee will I give it" (13:15). Prayer gives us the authority to claim the divine promises.
4. *It was the place of power.* "Arise, walk through the land" (13:17). In prayer we not only receive God's call but also His power to obey and follow Him fully.

Jacob, in his prayer with the wrestling angel, was on holy ground. His experience can guide our heart and mind as we come to take hold of God. In the agony of prayer, Jacob's strength failed him. At the end of his resources, he received the blessing of the "divine wrestler" (Gen. 32:26–29). (You will note with interest the lesson Hosea drew from Jacob's experience, as recorded in Hosea 12:4–6.)

Moses offered one of the boldest prayers in the Bible (Num. 14:17–24). Utterly self-forgetful, Moses pled the covenant promises of God. The divine response to such intercessory prayer was immediate. Other intercessions of Moses can guide our way in prayer, too. A study of Exodus 5:15–23 and 6:1–9 will show how he faced the trials of leadership.

1. Amid crisis and criticism, *Moses turned to God.* Nothing but trouble had come since he had approached Pharaoh: The promised deliverance had not taken place.
2. *Moses gained insight* into the infinite patience of God. Human impatience was met with divine patience.
3. *Moses received a great and satisfying answer.* "Now shalt thou see" (6:1). Amid the disheartening disappointments of his leadership, Moses learned that God was with him—if only he would follow God and be ready to do His will.

Hannah shows us a woman's prayer of thanksgiving and triumph (1 Sam. 1:26–28 and 2:1–3). What a great soul Hannah was! Her story is one of rare delicacy. Arising out of faith and hope, her prayer for a son was answered. She knew the secret and power of prayer. Trace these three aspects of Hannah's prayer.

1. She offered God a noble prayer of thanksgiving.
2. In her prayer song there was a solemn dedication.
3. Hannah expressed a heart-inspiring confession of faith.

Hezekiah is another whose prayer is worthy of emulation (Is. 37). Mark these stages:

1. He rent his clothes (v. 1), revealing deep concern.
2. He put on sackcloth (v. 1), showing true humiliation.
3. He went into the house of the Lord (v. 1), there to worship.

Then Hezekiah made confession (v. 3), expressed his hope (v. 4), spread his trouble before the Lord, (v. 14), and made his petition (v. 15).

Other prominent examples of prayer are those of *Isaac* (Gen. 25:21), *Job, Melchizedek* (Gen. 14:19,20), *Lot* (Gen. 19:19), *Manasseh* (2 Chr. 33:12), *Isaiah* (Is. 64), and others—all alike in fullness of faith in God.

A word must be said about *David,* who gives us no theoretical lessons about prayer but leads us right into "the prayer laboratory." No one in the Old Testament can teach us so much about our approach to God as David. How rich and varied were his prayers. Here is one of his matchless prayers, so apropos for a time like this, when the world is so topsy-turvy. Examining this priceless example in Psalm 3:1–8, we find six phases:

1. Communication with God (vv. 1,2)—diversity of foes, discouragement.
2. Consciousness of God (v. 3)—David is God-encircled.
3. Cry to God (vv. 4,5)—rest and refreshment to follow.
4. Confidence in God (v. 6)—prayer changed things.
5. Call upon God (v. 7)—courage, when prayerless, is foolish.
6. Confession about God (v. 8)—God is the Source of all salvation.

Prayers in the New Testament

Reaching the New Testament, we find it abounding in types and examples of prayer. It presents a gallery of prayer warriors, who blazed the way to a more exalted prayer life. With its richer and fuller revelation of divine truth, the New Testament brings us clearer light regarding the duty, privilege, and power of prayer.

In the Old Testament, God had a temple for His people; in the New Testament, He has a people as His temple. Under the gospel, the saints have superior advantages in their communication and communion with God. As we have related, Old Testament prayers were for the most part associated with temporal blessings. In the New Testament, saints are urged to pray for and seek after spiritual blessings. Specific instructions are given for the guidance of those seeking spiritual gifts and graces. Promises and assurances are cited for the purpose of inspiring the most timid with confidence.

A further advantage a Christian today has over the Old Testament saints is the privilege of presenting his petitions in the name of Jesus Christ. "Ask in my *name*" (John 14:13, italics added). "Hitherto have ye asked nothing in *my name*" (John 16:24, italics added). Ancient believers could pray, but not in the peerless name of Jesus, even though they were accepted by God through the *future* propitiatory sacrifice of Christ. They had "the spirit of faith" in the Savior to come. "Abraham rejoiced to see my day," said Christ.

Further, church saints have the added advantage of Christ's intercession on their behalf. He pledged Himself to act on behalf of His own as their personal intercessor. "I will·pray the Father for you." This was a completely new revelation, an announcement and an assurance no Old Testament believer ever had.

As a higher encouragement to His saints, Christ assures them that *He will Himself answer* their supplications. "Whatsoever ye shall ask in my name, *that will I do.*... If ye shall ask anything in my name, *I will do it.*"

Another advantage in prayer brought by the New Testament is the ministry of the Holy Spirit. The Jews of old knew very little about the third Person of the Trinity. It was the death, resurrection, and ascension of Christ that liberated the gift of the Spirit on our behalf. One purpose of His ministry is to awaken and keep alive within believers a spirit of prayer. The indispensable benefit of such a gift is that believers have the guarantee that their prayers are heard and answered as they pray in and by the Spirit.

Summarizing then the privileges of New Testament believers, what else can we do but exclaim, "Tis a broad land, of wealth unknown." Should not we, with all our advantages, have the same power with God as saints like Moses, Elijah, and Daniel had? How they could storm heaven and secure amazing results! What holy intimacy seemed to exist between them and God! With all our added privileges, our prayer life should be more vital and dynamic than in Old Testament days. But is it?

Our Lord's Example

It will certainly be profitable to observe several characteristic features of our Lord's prayer ministry.

1. He loved a solitary place for prayer (Mark 1:35, 6:46; John 6:15; and Matt. 14:23). Christ also believed in the morning watch. Do we?

2. He believed in praying for His enemies (Matt. 5:44 and Luke 6:28). At the cross He prayed for His murderers, the Romans and the Jews. The Romans were the immediate agents of His death; the Jews the instigators of it.

3. He abhorred mere show in prayer (Matt. 6:5,8). It is not the eloquence or length of our prayers but their quality that counts.

4. He believed in basic methods of prayer (Matt. 6:9). The so-called Lord's Prayer is a model prayer, unequaled for its beauty and comprehensiveness.

5. He sought for wisdom and guidance in solitude (Luke 6:12). Faced with the need to choose His disciples, Christ retired from the interruption of the world. "Cold mountains, and the midnight air, witness'd the fervor of His prayer." Have we learned that "devotional solitude is commended by high example and commanded by the high authority of the Savior?"

6. He advocated fervent, importunate prayer, (Luke 18:1–8 and James 5:16). Perseverence in prayer is advocated in the three key words: *ask, seek, knock.*

7. He taught that true humility should accompany prayer (Luke 18:9–13). Communication with God must be accompanied by lowliness of heart. If prayer is to be acceptable, it must rise from an altar on which pride has been the first sacrifice. If we would be accepted by God, as we pray we must shun the vainglory and offensive ostentation of the Pharisees.

8. He sought the will of God on His knees (Luke 22:39–44). The ruling passion of Christ's life was to know His Father's will and get it done.
9. His prayers were saturated with tears (Heb. 5:7). Perhaps our prayers are ineffectual because they are too dry.
10. He continues His prayer ministry in heaven (Heb. 4:14–16).

The Book of Acts, called by some the fifth gospel of the New Testament, is saturated with prayer. The early church was vibrantly dynamic in her witness. Why? She lived on her knees. The church was born in a prayer meeting; and living in such an atmosphere, she turned the world upside down (Acts 1:14). Read the Book of Acts! Whenever the saints prayed, something happened. (You may want to trace the following prayers and use them as a series for prayer-meeting meditations: Acts 1:14,24; 2:42; 3:1; 4:23–31; 6:4–7; 7:59,60; 8:15; 9:4–6,11,40; 10:2,9; 12:5,12; 14:23; 16:13,16,25; 21:5; and 27:35. The letters A–c–t–s can spell out the phases of prayer found in the book: Adoration, Confession, Thanksgiving, Supplication.)

The Prayers of Paul

Paul was preeminently a man of prayer. As soon as he was saved, he was found praying. He was strong in prayer and even turned a prison cell into a prayer chamber (Acts 16:25).

"Prayer is a creature's strength, his very breath and being." A study of Paul's life and labors proves that prayer was his "breath and being" more than it was for almost any other man. The apostle's prayers afford masterpieces of intercession unexcelled in the devotional literature of any age or country. A remarkable feature of Paul's prayers is that they are all conceived on the highest plane of spiritual living. They breathe the air of heaven and serve to lift our prayer life to a higher level too. Here is a brief list of Paul's matchless prayers, which is indicative of what he taught concerning prayer.

1. Prayer for a personal Pentecost (Eph. 3:13–21).
2. Prayer for perservance in godliness (Phil. 1:9–11).
3. Prayer for spiritual perception (Col. 1:9–13).
4. Prayer for perfection of faith and love (1 Thess. 3:9–13).
5. Prayer for complete sanctification (1 Thess. 5:23,24).
6. Prayer for the fulfillment of God's will (2 Thess. 1:11,12).
7. Prayer for deliverance from evil men (2 Thess. 3:1–5).

Saints at prayer in the days of Paul and the other apostles teach us what a Christian poet has beautifully expressed:

> *In every joy that crowns my days,*
> *In every pain I bear,*
> *My heart shall find delight in praise,*
> *Or seek relief in prayer.*

Another truth our hearts dare not miss is that if we would be heard and answered as we pray, we must live in harmony with our daily supplications. Our person and performance should not contradict our prayer.

Studying the prayer examples of the Bible, we arrive at the conclusion that one of the greatest assets of prayer is its character-training power. The life of the pray-er, and those prayed for, undergoes a change. Take, for instance, the prayers of Paul. Consistently he kept Christian character in view. Read Ephesians 1:16–23; 3:4–21; Philippians 1:9–11; Colossians 1:9–12; and 1 Thessalonians 3:11–13. Here you will see what kind of men and women such prayers would produce. Prayer is valueless if it is not character-forming.

Throughout the New Testament, prayer is proved to be a mighty force. "The prayer of faith moves the hand of Him that moveth all things." May grace be ours to appropriate, as the apostles did, the power which prayer can deliberate in and through our lives!

10

The Scope of Prayer

While God's ear is universal, it is also endlessly discrim-inating. Some petitions, because of their nature or because of the life of the petitioner, are never answered. Prayer, does, however, cover all persons, places, and particulars. It is a shortcut to the heart of God; therefore, we should be as universal as we wish in our prayers. We can pray "with *all* prayer... with *all* perseverance and supplication for *all* saints" (Eph. 6:18, italics added). It is always safe to inter-cede for others: No one is too poor to offer such a gift, and no one is so wealthy that he could give a richer gift. The scope of prayer is vast. We can

- pray for all men (1 Tim. 2:1).
- pray about all things (John 15:16).
- pray for all saints (Eph. 6:18).
- pray for Israel (Rom. 10:1).
- pray for laborers to harvest (Luke 10:2).
- pray for rulers (1 Tim. 2:2).
- prayer for ministers (Eph. 6:19).
- pray for conversions (1 Tim. 2:1,4).
- pray for pardon after discovered sin (1 John 1:9).
- pray for sick believers (James 5:16).

• pray that the Spirit will show us how to pray (Rom. 8:26).

In this chapter we will endeavor to discover in greater detail how the scope of prayer covers the personal, social, material, natural, spiritual, ecclesiastical, and national realms. When referring to prayer, the terms "everything," "all things," and "anything" are absolutely all-inclusive in their scope (Phil. 4:6, Matt. 21:22, and John 14:14). Beyond these realms we cannot go. Prayers may relate to all that we can see in the world around us. However, our prayers do have a temporary limitation.

As we seek to outline the scope of prayer, we may wonder how God can possibly listen to countless millions all over the world who, in numerous languages, present their own praises, needs, cares, sorrows, and problems. A distinguishing characteristic of the greatest human minds is the ability to be aware of and to understand vast concepts and still pay attention to minute details. Thus it is with God and, of course, much more so. He names the stars and heals the brokenhearted (Ps. 147:3,4). Nothing escapes His all-encompassing gaze or eludes His infinite comprehension. God's comprehension cannot be overloaded.

When we take advantage of the promise, "whatsoever ye ask," we must, though, leave the answer to Him. Our prayers are responded to not always as we wish, but as He knows best. God never fails to give the very best to those who leave the choice with Him. "The Lord's choice is always *choice.*" Let us, then, "in the presence of our Lord bosom all our cares" and act on the advice of Hartley Coleridge: "If for any wish thou dar'st not pray, pray for grace to cast that wish away."

The Personal Realm

Afflicted as we are with so many personal cares and needs, the bulk of our prayers are related to ourselves. The old Negro spiritual says, "I'm standin' in the need o' prayer, O Lord." Isn't it wonderful that we can retire to our place of solitude and talk with the Lord about all that concerns us? "He shall call upon me, and I will answer him" (Ps. 91:15).

- Are you in trouble? Then claim God's promises (Ps. 50:15 and 86:7).
- Do you have a financial problem? You can claim divine relief (Ps. 69:33 and 102:17; Phil. 4:19).
- Are you facing some peril and require protection? Plead Psalms 32:6,7 and 91:1–7.
- Are you in doubt, needing guidance and direction in a choice that must be made? You should claim Isaiah 30:19–21 and Jeremiah 33:3.
- Do you have a conscience disturbed because of personal sin? It is blessed to know that you can tell it all to Him, who offers to pardon and deliver (Is. 55:6 and Rom. 10:13).

Charlotte Elliott well expressed the benefits of prayer in these lines.

Lord, till I reach yon blissful shore,
No privilege so dear shall be
As thus my inmost soul to pour
In prayer to Thee!

A baby cries to attract attention, to get what he wants. Personal prayer must not be used thus. The prodigal son prayed twice, "Give me" and "make me." Both requests were graciously answered. But we should be grateful that God does not always answer our personal, unworthy prayers. Self is an intruder, even in the secret place, and our prayers too often are motivated by a desire to realize our own wishes! In His mercy, God sometimes answers our prayers, although they may not be on a very high level (Judges 16:28). He listens, even though we do not know the ramifications of what we are asking for (Mark 10:35–45).

When we center prayer on our petty, individual problems and try to use God for our own ends, prayer is futile. Prayers said for ourselves must have as their end an increase in the value of the life we would give others. Jesus could pray, "For their sakes *I* sanctify *myself.*" Closet prayer should lead to world service.

The Social Realm

Many of our prayers are answered through others; therefore we must pray for others. A person's prayer life is always enriched when he prays for others. Paul prayed often for others (Rom. 1:9, Phil. 1:4, and Eph. 1:15,16). Christ exemplified this practice, too (Matt. 19:13). We must not only pray with others, but for others. Selfish prayer shuts others out, because it shuts God out. Unselfish prayers are ever rich in intercession, adoration, and grace. How blessed we are when we make mention of others in our prayers. William Horner wrote in *Let Us Pray,* "The less we pray for ourselves and the more we pray for others, the nearer we will approach the spiritual conception of true prayer, and the greater assurance we will have that our prayers will be answered."

Prayer for others is the noblest type of prayer. Clarence

Macartney reminds us that "the first prayer recorded in the Bible, the prayer of Abraham, was a prayer for others, his intercession for the cities of the plain. The last words of Christ to His disciples before His crucifixion were a prayer that they might be kept in the truth and from the evil that is in the world. Paul, when he knelt on the sands of Miletus, having finished all his ministry for the church at Ephesus, poured out his soul in intercession for the elders of that church."

In his chapter on "Praying for Others," Macartney tells us that such praying has a twofold benefit. First, prayer for others lifts the man who prays out of himself and brings to view the glories of life. Second, prayer for others benefits those for whom we pray.

The most conspicuous saints of the Bible practiced intercessory prayer. We have Job (42:7–10), Moses (Ex. 8:12,30; 9:33), Samuel (1 Sam. 15:11), Elijah (James 5:17,18), Ezra (9:5–15), Nehemiah (1:4–11), Jeremiah (7:16 and 14:11), Paul (Rom. 1:9 and Phil. 1:3–11), Stephen (Acts 7:60), and Epaphras (Col. 4:12). Our blessed Lord continues this type of praying in heaven (Heb. 7:25).

Intercessory prayer brings us into "the royal priesthood" (1 Pet. 2:5,9). How privileged we are to be associated with such a holy group! This is a ministry which many can exercise who are unable to perform other aspects of Christian service, those who may be invalids, infirm, or aged. Eternity alone will reveal what has been accomplished through the prayers of God's shut-in saints.

One of the marvelous features of social praying is that it reaches persons and places who could not be covered in any other way. It is the shortest route to reach the uttermost parts of the earth.

Our friends and relatives, as objects of our intercession,

were probably in the mind of Peter in his first epistle (3:7;
see also Luke 11:5–8). Many of us owe more than we
understand to those who are bound to us by human ties.
Their prayers surround our life and service, and greatly
influence both. Archbishop Trench wrote beautifully of this
aspect of our prayer ministry.

> *When hearts are full of yearning tenderness*
> *For the loved absent, whom we cannot reach*
> *By deed or token, gesture, or kind speech,*
> *The spirit's true affection to express,*
> *Then, like a cup capacious to contain*
> *The overflowing of the heart, is prayer.*

We are apt to forget that prayers for our enemies are also
definitely enjoined in Scripture, both by precept and example
(Matt. 5:44, Luke 23:34, Acts 7:60, and 2 Tim. 4:16).

One day Joseph Parker, of the renowned City Temple,
London, was preaching in Hyde Park when an infidel tried
to shout him down with the question, "What did Christ do
for Stephen when he was stoned?" Parker answered immediately, "He gave him grace to pray for those who stoned
him." What a victory was Stephen's! Many believe that the
dying prayers of Stephen for his murderers resulted in the
conversion of Saul of Tarsus, who later became Paul the
Apostle.

There are three principles to guide those who engage in
intercessory prayer.

1. They must have a sincere desire for the highest interests of those for whom they pray.
2. They must have the utmost faith in God's promise and
   sufficiency to meet the needs of those prayed for.

3. They must hold themselves in readiness to cooperate in action as an outcome of their prayers. Such prayers take feet and go to those who are interceded for.

The Material Realm

Because we are made of the dust, we need much that comes from the dust to maintain us. Food, money, clothing, and other material necessities: Can we pray about these? Well, Jesus taught His own to pray, "Give us this day our daily bread." When George Mueller needed bread and milk for his orphans, he never told anyone of his need. It was his principle that God alone should be informed. God was already cognizant of what the orphans required, and Mueller believed that all he had to do was ask—and receive.

Was not our Lord thinking of food and clothing when He spoke of the sparrows and lilies? Yes, He is able to supply *all* our needs, even the most basic of our physical wants. The Bible shows many examples of His care. He miraculously fed the Israelites for forty years. He saw that his hungry prophet, Elijah, was supplied with food, even though it meant commissioning a raven to bring it. Our physical needs are not any less important to our loving Father.

The Natural Realm

Prayer is not merely a devotional exercise, but a dynamic force, one which brings us into contact with God the Creator, the all-beneficent One. Martin Tupper speaks of prayer as "the tender nerve that moves the muscles of Omnipotence."

While this type of prayer does not change God's plans, it

does provide the means for carrying them out. It removes the obstacles on our part, enabling God to perform His work. Prayer links human impotence with divine omnipotence and brings the infinite resources of the infinite God into beneficial action. Prayer becomes, as Tennyson put it, "a breath that fleets beyond this iron world, and touches Him that made it."

Whether we think of the miracles God performed for the Israelites—the subduing of kingdoms and turning of enemies to flight, the closing of the mouths of lions, the quenching of fire, the experiences of an Elijah, a Gideon, a Samson, the sun standing still, Jonah and the whale—or the miracles of Jesus, the story is the same: God is able to accomplish great and mighty things on behalf of His own. Since He is the Creator, all laws are subject to His bidding.

The Spiritual Realm

Prayers related to sins and struggles in the spiritual realm abound in the Bible. Jacob at the brook (Gen. 32), Job and his mystery (Job 14), David and his dark sin (Ps. 51:3–9), and many others. When a person is conscious of sin, "confession is a fundamental element of prayer," says Ella Robertson. "There are times, too, when confession to some fellowman is what is needed to clear up our spiritual condition." Confession may have to be on a personal level (2 Sam. 12; Ps. 51; 1 John 1:7–9) or be undertaken for an entire nation, an action which occurred during the ministry of Ezra (Ezra 9). That peace follows confession to God and to others is amply proved in Psalm 32.

Under this section we can briefly discuss prayer and temptation (Matt. 26:41). We are not to pray that temptation may be kept from us, but that we may be preserved from the evil lurking in the midst of any temptation. Temptation is a universal experience. Temptations may differ according to our heredity, environment, and age, but they come to all. Clarence Macartney wrote,

There are temptations of the body, temptations of the mind, temptations of the spirit. Temptation is a great equalizer. It smites in youth: it smites in middle life: even the aged are not exempt from its cruel and dangerous sorrows, for

> *The gray-haired saint may fall at last,*
> *The surest guide a wanderer prove;*
> *Death only binds us fast*
> *To that bright shore of love.*

Temptation is a sleepless, unwearying enemy. . . . Great is the power of temptation, and great is the destructive power of a single temptation. . . . A single temptation not fought against with the divinely appointed weapon can ruin a character that has been slowly and painfully built through long years.

It is because of the fact, power, and danger of temptation that Jesus urged us to watch and pray. Watching and praying are practically equivalent; for when we are watching against temptation, we are praying against it; and when we are praying against it, we are on guard against it. When we pray, we bring ourselves into vital contact with Christ, who knows all about the wiles and stratagems of the devil. He met this enemy and triumphed gloriously over him; therefore, He is able to make us more than conquerors too.

A British pilot had not flown very far from his base before he noticed a peculiar noise. Looking down, he saw a rat gnawing away at a vital part of his plane. He could not stop to kill the rodent. What could he do? Up into the rarified air he zoomed and, starved for oxygen, the rat rolled over dead. Does this not illustrate the power of prayer? When the rat of hell tempts us, prayer takes us up into the rare air of heaven, where everything not of God quickly dies.

The Ecclesiastical Realm

Everything related to church life comes within the scope of prayer. Many New Testament prayers were taken up with the concerns and character of the church of Jesus Christ. Paul's prayers for the churches he founded are even now rich in example and suggestion. The carnal Corinthians, the legalized Galatians, the confused Colossians, the troubled Thessalonians—all alike were surrounded with the apostle's mighty intercessions. The care of all the churches was his, but Paul knew how to cast such a burden upon the Lord. He prayed for all the churches to abound in love, to stand fast, to grow in grace, to pray without ceasing. Paul never sinned by ceasing to pray for those whom God had helped him to win.

God wants us to pray for the deepening of the church's spiritual life. Revival is meant for the church (Ps. 85:6). Revival brings the church into fuller fellowship with the Lord, who desires to use it in a world of need. The salvation of souls is the direct outcome of such a revival.

Samuel Zwemer, in writing strikingly about prayer and missions, proves conclusively that the evangelization of the lost at home and abroad depends upon a revival of prayer within the church. "Since the beginning of the missionary enterprise, in the upper room at Jerusalem, prayer has been

78

the secret of power, perseverance, and victory. The history of missions is the history of answered prayer." We have received the entreaty of Jesus to pray to the Lord of the harvest to gather in the multitudes in darkness—both at home and in the regions beyond. Let us do so without delay.

The National Realm

A casual reading of the Scriptures is sufficient to show how prayer is vitally associated with communal, national, and international affairs. Frank Laubach writes of "prayer minute-men—a minute a day—to flash thousands of instantaneous prayers at people far and near."

In Scripture, kings are found praying for themselves, for the people they rule, and for their enemies. All persons in authority, including national leaders, are to be prayed for (Ezra 6:10, Jer. 29:7, and 1 Tim. 2:2). If ever our rulers needed the prayers of God's people and needed to pray for wisdom themselves, it is now. How confused the leaders must be! How impotent they are in solving the gigantic international problems facing them. They are seemingly unable to carry out any ideas they may have for world peace. This topsy-turvy world certainly needs our prayers.

Hosea gives us a pattern of national prayer, but he suggests the utter futility of such prayer if it is not followed by national righteousness and the will to do God's will (Hos. 6:1–3). Some years ago *Life* magazine carried a remarkable editorial on "Why Men Pray," from which the following words are culled.

During an impasse at the Constitutional Convention in June 1787, Benjamin Franklin addressed the chairman (George

Washington) as follows: "The small progress we have made . . . is, methinks, a melancholy proof of the imperfection of the human understanding. . . . I have lived, sir, a long time, and the longer I live, the more convincing proofs I see of this truth, *that God governs in the affairs of men.* And if a sparrow cannot fall to the ground without His notice, is it probable that an empire can rise without His aid? We have been assured, sir, in the Sacred Writings, that "except the Lord build the house, they labor in vain that build it." I firmly believe this; and I also believe that, without His concurring aid, we shall succeed in political building no better than the builders of Bable." Franklin then moved that daily prayers be offered before the Assembly again got down to business. The motion was lost, but not because these men did not believe in prayer. To avoid sectarian controversy and for other practical reasons, they preferred to pray in private. But they prayed.

11

The Agony of Prayer

Very few of us know much about wrestling prayer. We may even find prayer to be pleasing and profitable, but certainly not painful. It is an easy exercise, never exhausting. Often, we rejoice over the access prayer affords, but we are strangers to its agony. Prayer may take up a little of our time, but we never lose any blood, sweat, or tears over it.

Now, God does not expect us to agonize over those things we need. All we have to do is simply to ask, lovingly and truthfully. Desperation, shouting, frenzy are not necessary as we come as children to our heavenly Father for the necessities of life. He is loving, kind, and generous—more willing to bless than we are to be blessed. He "giveth to all men liberally, and upbraideth not" (James 1:5). As the omniscient One, He knows all about our needs; and without coercion, without much loud speaking, He will meet them.

There are times, however, when prayer should be agony. In Gethsemane, our Lord agonized in prayer. His supplications were sometimes saturated with anguish and tears. There were occasions when, as He prayed, He groaned in the spirit. When Jesus faced the powers of darkness, the hardness of men, the weakness of the flesh, prayer was more than communion for Him; it was a grim conflict. Scripture records, too, that the Holy Spirit groans in prayer.

The word *strive,* which Paul often used in connection with prayer, is closely related in the Greek to our English term *agonize.* He desired the saints at Rome to "strive" in prayer for him (Rom. 15:30). Up against fierce satanic opposition in Asia, crushed and despairing even of life, Paul sought the tense, wrestling intercessory prayers of those who loved him in the Lord. And such prayers prevailed on his behalf. Paul wanted God's children, upon whose prayers he relied, to labor with him in prayer for three things: "That I might be delivered from them that are disobedient"; "That my ministrations may be acceptable"; "That I may come to you in joy, through the will of God."

Paul used the same expression about Epaphras who was always *striving* for the saints that they might "stand perfect and complete in all the will of God" (Col. 4:12). Writing to the Colossians, Paul reminded them of his spiritual burden and anguish in their behalf. "I would that ye knew what great conflict I have for you, . . . and for as many as have not seen my face in the flesh" (Col. 2:1).

The mightiest prayer warriors through the ages have been those who experienced something of the agony of Christ and of Paul in prayer. They shared the determination of Jacob who, as he wrestled, cried, "I will not let thee go unless thou bless me." Here are some examples:

- John Fletcher stained the walls of his room by the breath of his frequent, earnest prayers.
- John Welch, whose wife complained when she found him prostrate in prayer, replied, "O woman, I have the

souls of three thousand to answer for, and I know not how it is with many of them!''

• Henry Martyn, lamenting that "want of private devotional reading and shortness of prayer through incessant sermon-making had produced much strangeness between God and his soul,'' was yet characterized by much fervor in prayer.

• Payson, we are told by his biographer, wore the hardwood boards into grooves, where his knees pressed so often and so long in ardent and perservering prayer.

• William Bramwell, famous English Methodist preacher, would often spend as much as four hours agonizing in a single season of prayer. No wonder he traveled his circuit as a flame of fire.

• John Wesley also knew something of these hell-shaking prayers. "Give me one hundred preachers who fear nothing but sin and desire nothing but God, and I care not a straw whether they be clergymen or laymen; such alone will shake the gates of Hell and set up the kingdom of heaven on earth. God does nothing but in answer of prayer.''

In O. Hallesby's heart-warming volume *Prayer*, two telling chapters explain the kind of prayer which involves anguish and suffering. The author asks, "Why should our prayer-life be a constantly flowing source of anguish?'' His answers are remarkable.

He states that a strenuous, powerful prayer life becomes the target of satanic antagonism. The devil knows the effect of such praying upon his kingdom and mobilizes everything that he can commandeer in order to destroy wrestling prayers. Then, as Dr. Hallesby says, the devil "has an excellent confederate in our bosoms: our old Adam.'' And how powerfully this old nature rebels against any form of prayer, especially the form of prayer we are now considering. Our carnal nature is full of enmity toward God and hates everything related to the spiritual life. Thus with the devil and the flesh against us, victory over principalities, powers, and the spiritual hosts of wickedness requires the wrestling in prayer which Paul not only wrote of but experienced (Eph. 6:12).

Let these weighty words sink into your mind: "Everyone who is experienced in prayer knows that to listen quietly and humbly for what the Spirit of prayer says requires continued and powerful wrestling. It requires wrestling in the first place in order to hear and obey the Spirit's admonitions to prayer. Indeed, it involves both wrestling and watching, as Jesus said in Mark 4:38, because the spirit is willing to pray, but the flesh is weak. Further, 'a struggle is involved in listening to what the Spirit has to say also while we pray.'''

Then Hallesby points out, and rightly so, that this kind of praying is often misunderstood. "It has been conceived of as a struggle in prayer against God, the thought being that God withholds His gifts as long as possible," and they have to be wrung from Him. Such a conception of "wrestling in prayer is pagan and not Christian." Our bountiful God needs no persuasion to meet His children's needs. Our striving is a struggle, not with God, but with the devil and ourselves. Satanic hostility, our selfishness, slothfulness, lethargy, and ignorance concerning the true import of prayer— all alike demand striving, persevering prayer, prayer which faints not but continues steadfastly until victory is won.

In linking fasting to prayer, Jesus introduced His disciples to the great struggle connected with such a privileged exercise (Mark 9:29). Fasting, an outward act which should be carried out only when there is an inner need of it (Matt. 9:14,15), involves more than abstinence from food and drink for a short or long period of time. It implies "voluntary abstinence for a long time from various necessities of life, such as food, drink, rest, association with people, and so forth."

The New Testament clearly teaches that fasting is related to fierce temptations, to the making of a decision or choice, to the planning and carrying out of very difficult tasks. Such fasting is necessary so that believing prayer can yield the needed wisdom, guidance, and power from God. "Fasting," says Hallesby, "helps to give us that inner sense of spiritual penetration by means of which we can discern clearly that for which the Spirit of prayer would have us pray in exceptionally difficult circumstances."

The distressed, confused plight of the world; the low spiritual condition of the church; the carnality and unspirituality of the average professing Christian; the multitudes dying in heathern darkness—all these demand that we stir ourselves from ignorance or distaste for wrestling prayer.

Prayers that shake heaven, confound hell, compel the world to turn to God are not the short, heartless, insipid prayers we are content with now. They must be prayers motivated by the heartbeat of God and the passion and compassion of Calvary. They must approximate, in some measure, the blood-stained, tear-soaked prayers of Him to whom prayer was wrestling as well as worship.

12

The Power of Prayer

The prayers of the righteous have helped to shape the history of the world. In prayer men grasp the hand that controls all things. With the exercise of prayer, contact is made with the Creator of the ends of the earth. This is why it is true that "Satan trembles when he sees the weakest saint upon his knees."

If, however, we are not mighty in prayer and do not believe that prayer is the greatest unused spiritual asset in the world, then the power of heaven will never be released through our lives. If anyone is cognizant of the power of prayer, it is the devil. That is why he strives in every possible way to weaken our prayer aspirations and activities.

While the question, "Does God answer prayer?" is one of perennial interest, we have no need to stop and prove that He does. It has been computed that out of 667 Bible prayers for specific things, there are 454 traceable answers. The Psalms carry numerous allusions to the fact of the power of prayer. Joshua's testimony supporting the proposition, and also that of Solomon, has been abundantly verified by the saints of every age (Josh. 23:14 and 1 Kings 8:23,24,56).

Scattered throughout the previous pages of this book are

evidences that prayer is the mightiest force in the world. Let us now try to summarize how this dynamic power has operated in the lives of the saints of God for whom, as they prayed, God performed. The spiritual giants who have shaken the kingdom of darkness have been men of effectual prayer. They did not spend too much of their time studying prayer; *they prayed*. Across the pages of Scripture and of church history we trace the records of those who, in bold, holy faith, pleaded with God and were heard.

Prayer has produced marvelous results in the lives of multitudes. When they laid hold of God, God laid hold of them, and something happened. What a wealth of testimony they have left us in support of the power of prayer! How convincing are their answers to prayer! They came boldly to the throne of grace, and were not sent away empty:

- Abraham prayed long for a son: Isaac came.
- Eliezer prayed for guidance: Rebekah appeared.
- Jacob prayed: His brother's attitude was changed.
- Moses prayed: Heaven's wrath was subdued.
- Josua prayed: Achan was discovered and Ai destroyed.
- Hannah prayed: Samuel was given to her.
- Elijah prayed: The heavens were shut and opened.
- Elisha prayed: Drought came and a dead child lived again.
- David prayed: Ahithophel, the traitor, hanged himself.
- Jehoshaphat prayed: His enemies were routed.
- Hezekiah prayed: 185,000 Assyrians were slain.
- Daniel prayed. Archangels were set in motion.

True prayer releases divine forces and restrains evil forces.

• Jesus prayed: The pillars of the church were chosen.
• The disciples prayed: Pentecost became a mighty factor.
• The early church prayed: Peter was liberated from prison.

Documentation of the power of prayer did not disappear when the last page of inspired canon was filled.

• Savonarola prayed: A city was won for God.
• Martin Luther prayed: God broke the spell of ages.
• John Knox prayed: Tyrants were terrified and Scotland was blessed.
• George Whitefield prayed: A thousand souls were saved in one day.
• George Fox prayed: The great Quaker movement was born.
• George Mueller prayed: Hungry orphans were fed.
• Hudson Taylor prayed: Inland China was evangelized.

On we could go, citing thousands of witnesses, all proving the lengths to which God will go when men and women are prepared to lay hold of Him and refuse to let Him go until He blesses. The consistent witness of Bible and church saints is that prayer is the highest resource of the soul. Subjected to trials, sorrows, failures, and sin, these men and women yet experienced the transforming power of prayer. Foes, adverse circumstances, weaknesses, moods— all were conquered.

We ought always to pray and not to faint, since prayer's mighty power fulfills the needs of the body; covers the cares of the home; enables us to face heavy responsibilities; empowers us for Christian service; triumphs over hostile, satanic forces; and changes circumstances, sinners, and saints.

Prayer is an instrument of God whereby He liberates power in the realms of nature and in the storehouse of grace—both in our behalf. We have, for example, the following reasons for the power of prayer.

1. Christ's revelation of God the Father as the all-sovereign One: He taught about God as the heavenly Father who loves and cares.
2. The Father is never a prisoner in His own world, bound by laws of His own creation. He is the God of the impossible.
3. The finished work of Christ made possible access and boldness of our approach to the Father. Redemption bought this privilege.
4. The Holy Spirit, the Spirit of power who is also fully God, is the saint's Enabler and Inspirer as he intercedes for others.
5. The vast family of God, with varied experiences trustworthy in character, mighty through God to the pulling down of strongholds, have left records that cannot be disputed. They were not deceived, and their declared achievements by prayer are not based upon falsehood.
6. Rich Bible promises encourage us to lay hold of God and prove how willing and ready He is to accomplish whatever we ask of Him, as long as what we plead for is in accordance with His blessed will.

Do we know how to pray in such a way as to receive answers? Do we deem the silence of God to our prayers as one of the most dreadful things we could experience? Do we believe that prayer can do the following?

1. *Sanctify the supplicant.* Prayer purifies the life. "Praying will either make a man leave off sinning, or else sinning will make a man leave off praying." As we pray, we will grow in grace. Prayer "stretches the sinews of the soul and hardens its muscles." Prayer creates an inward joy nothing can disturb (John 16:24).
2. *Glorify the supplicant.* Secret prayer brings open reward (Matt. 6:6). As the life becomes the channel through which God's power is released, the pray-er, shunning all self-glorification, ascribes all glory to God, since all power is His.

Long ago John Newton taught us to sing:

> *My soul, ask what thou wilt,*
> *Thou canst not be too bold;*
> *Since His own blood for thee was spilt*
> *What else can He withhold?*
> *Beyond thine utmost wants,*
> *His love and power can bless;*
> *To praying souls He always grants*
> *More than they can express.*

May we, too, be named among God's prayer warriors, able to subdue kingdoms, stop the mouths of lions, and put to flight the enemies of God. As the world totters from crisis to crisis, we have so much to pray for. Prayer can prevail for our nation's leaders, educators, our military forces, our poor, the hungry, the prisoners, the multitudes living in darkness, for ourselves. That all-necessary faith, hope, and courage may be ours as we await the coming of the Bridegroom.

13

The Problems of Prayer

Although simplicity is the essence of prayer, prayer does present difficulties and problems which some minds find hard to cope with. There are those who seem to be baffled by the exercise, laws, and results of prayer. Because this is a most important and intensely practical aspect of this discussion, let us seek to clarify many prayer "problems."

The Problem of Natural Order

Sophisticated men, like Kant the philosopher, for example, think it "absurd and presumptuous" to ask favors of God. It is considered arrogant to ask God to alter His cosmic plans to satisfy man's wishes. The universe is looked upon as a "closed system, fixed unalterably by natural law, a system in which nothing but foregone conclusions can happen." Thus prayer is contrary to the reign of law in nature. One is impertinent to expect that the through traffic on the highways of the laws of nature can be side-tracked to a country lane by our puny petitions.

Modern science has revealed, however, that such a problem is purely artificial. The universe is not closed. Laws still reign within the universe, but "amid and through these laws are open possibilities, open to initiative and to creative faith.'' Natural law used to say that nothing heavier than air could withstand the force of gravity. Now airplanes weighing tons speed through the air, and rockets blast into the heavens, bearing man as far as the moon.

The renowned jurist, Justice Holmes, once said, ''The mode in which the inevitable comes to pass is through effort.'' The witness of Scripture and history is that if God's plans are inevitable, man's voluntary prayers can still be part of the effort on which He counts to fulfill them. It is upon this paradox that our Christian faith is built. Those who believe in the reality, possibility, and power of prayer worship a God who knows and foresees all, yet ''whose service is perfect freedom.'' To them, God is greater than all the laws He created and can command any one of them to obey His will on behalf of His redeemed children.

The Problem of Wrong Approach

Scripture is plain that God does hear and answer prayer. His ear is never so distant that it cannot hear the right kind of petition (Is. 59:1). We are urged to pray at all times, in all places, for all needs. It is essential to believe that God is a rewarder of all who diligently seek Him. The scope of His promise is

- without limit of place: ''Pray everywhere'' (1 Tim. 2:8).
- without limit of time: ''Always'' (Luke 18:1).
- without limit of subject: ''Everything'' (Phil. 4:6).

Whether our requirements are sacred or secular, spiritual or material, God waits to grant us those things we desire of

Him. He assures us of His constant care and concern and that there is "no place where earth's sorrows are more felt, than up in heaven."

But while all of this is so, God only answers our prayers when they are presented in the way of His appointing and according to His superior intelligence. Answered prayer, then, depends upon the right approach to the throne of grace. Prayer will never be sound and normal unless we pray aright. Prayer has its laws, which must be known and obeyed.

Hallesby enlarges on some of the errors to guard against if prayer is to be effective. One of these concerns the idea that we must help God fulfill our petitions. All He asks of us is to *pray*. He carries the responsibility of hearing and fulfilling our prayers.

Neither do we have to pray in order to make God kind and good to answer our prayer. God is ever good and grants us what we need of His own accord. He is love, and the essence of love is giving. Prayer, then, is "not for the purpose of making God good or generous. He is that from all eternity. . . . Prayer has one function, and that is to answer 'Yes' when He knocks, to open the soul and give Him the opportunity to bring us the answer."

We also pray amiss when we make use of prayer for the purpose of commanding God to do our bidding. Some arrogant, demanding prayers are an insult to the Almighty. He is not an inferior to whom orders are to be issued. Says Hallesby, "God has not given us His promises and the privilege of prayer in order that we might use them to pound a demanding fist upon the table before God and compel Him to do what we ask." We violate the governing laws of prayer if we thus compel Him to answer us.

A further misuse of prayer is that of trying to make use of

God for our own personal advantage and enjoyment. Selfishness, even in a Christian, knows no bounds. The carnal nature desires everything for itself. We are given an example of misused and unanswered prayer in Matthew 20:20–23. When the mother of James and John asked Jesus if her sons could sit on either side of His throne, Jesus answered, "Ye know not what ye ask." She surely did not. Selfish prayers have been humorously ridiculed in these well-known lines.

> *Lord bless me and my wife,*
> *My son Tom, and his wife,*
> *Us four—*
> *No more. Amen!*

Prayer in the name of Jesus Christ our Lord involves correspondence with His will and harmony with His wishes (Acts 19:13–16). In radio communication, the transmitting and receiving sets must be tuned to the same channel. So with prayer: There must be sympathy with the Lord's plans and purpose. Presenting our petitions in Christ's name is equivalent to coming before God with Christ's authority. The power of prayer depends upon the right use of the Name above every other name. Bearing His name implies likeness to His character. Employment of His name means identity of interests—union with Christ in His will and ways.

Hallesby remarks that "to pray in the name of Jesus is, in all likelihood, the deepest mystery in prayer. . . . Scripture speaks of the 'mystery of Christ' (Eph. 3:4). The name of Jesus is the greatest mystery in heaven and on earth. In heaven, this mystery is known; on earth it is unknown to most people. No one can fathom it fully. . . . To pray in the name of Jesus is the real element of prayer in our prayers. It is the helpless soul's helpless look unto a gracious Friend. The wonderful results which attend prayer of this kind can be accounted for only by the fact that we have opened the door unto Jesus and given Him access to our helplessness.''

The "If" of Faith

"Jesus answered and said unto them, Verily I say unto you, *If* ye have faith, and doubt not, ye shall not only do this which is done to the fig tree, but also *if* ye shall say unto this mountain, Be thou removed, and be thou cast into the sea; it shall be done. And all things, whatsoever ye shall ask in prayer, believing, ye shall receive" (Matt. 21:21,22, italics added).

As faith is the only means of communication with the invisible God, it is essential to the offering and answering of prayer (Heb. 11:6 and James 1:6,7). In prayer "all things are possible to him that believeth" (Mark 9:23). Great faith results in great blessing (Matt. 8:10,13 and 15:28). While prayer is the key to all the treasures of heaven, faith is the hand using that key.

Our Lord wants us to have the kind of faith that enables us to believe that He has answered our prayers, *before* the answer is received (Mark 11:14,20,23,24 and John 11:40,41). The threadbare story of the minister calling for a day of prayer for rain to relieve a drought afflicting the community comes to mind. A Sunday was chosen for such a day, and what a day—brilliant sunshine, with not a cloud on the horizon! A maiden turned up on the sunny Sunday with an umbrella under her arm. Several members chided the girl for bringing an umbrella to church on such a bright, cloudless day. "Well," she said, "we were told to come and pray for rain, and we must believe that God will send it." Before the service was over, we are told, the rain appeared, and the girl went home under her umbrella, the happiest church member of all. Others got soaked, but she reached home dry. Prayer had been mixed with faith.

The "If" of Abiding

"*If* ye abide in me, and my words abide in you, ye shall ask what ye will, and it shall be done unto you" (John 15:7, italics added).

Habitual obedience to all of God's commands is also closely related to effective prayer. How useless it is to pray if we refuse to do all the Lord requires of us! Prayer can only be acceptable to Him as it ascends from an obedient heart (Prov. 1:24–31, Zech. 7:12,13 and 1 John 3:22). "Our obedience," says William Proctor, "does not in itself merit an answer to our prayer, but it is a test of our fitness to receive it, and an indispensable qualification for our obtaining our petitions."

We recognize the fact that we have a permanent standing in Christ which nothing can affect. Union with Him can never be severed, but communion can. Thus, to abide in Christ means to have no known, unconfessed sin blocking communion with Him. Power in prayer is dependent upon such unbroken fellowship with Christ (Is. 59:1,2).

In our Lord's teaching there are two conditions which must be met before prayer can be answered (John 15:1–14): We must abide in Him and have His words abiding in us. The latter means more than memorizing verses. We must meditate upon Christ's words until they become part and parcel of our life. It is only then that they strengthen us by giving our faith its warrant and its plea.

The "If" of God's Will

"And this is the confidence that we have in him, that, *if* we ask any thing according to his will, he heareth us: And if we know that he hear us, whatsoever we ask, we know that we have the petitions that we desired of him" (1 John 5:14,15, italics added).

John, in very simple, understandable language, assured us that all prayers which are according to God's will are sure of being heard and answered. The sequence is clear: "Ask according to His will, and God will hear." Harmony with God's will, then, is not only an essential stipulation, but a necessary safeguard to our freedom in prayer. Christ's prayers were always offered in full submission to the will of His Father (Matt. 26:39,42 and John 12:27,28). Alas, our own prayers are often marred by petulant self-will! We do not pray in line with God's will but in line with our own will.

The confidence John speaks of is not associated with the obtaining of specific things asked for, but the obtaining of answers in accordance with God's perfect wisdom and infinite love.

A difficulty confronting many is, "What is the will of God? Is it something secret? If so, then we can never have the confidence of asking which John speaks about. How can we know we are praying according to His will?"

Such a will is revealed in a threefold way:

1. *By the written Word.* The broad principles of God's will are not to be found in isolated texts, but in the Scriptures as a whole.
2. *By the Holy Spirit.* As a member of the Godhead, He knows the will of God and is cognizant of all that concerns Christ. If prayerfully depended upon, the Spirit will enable us to discern between the divine will and our own will and feelings.
3. *By circumstances.* Sanctified common sense is not to be used only in deciding what is or is not of God. Discovering His will, we must seek grace and strength to fulfill it.

The "If" of Agreement

"Again I say unto you, That *if* two of you shall agree on earth as touching any thing that they shall ask, it shall be done for them of my Father which is in heaven. For where two or three are gathered together in my name, there am I in the midst of them" (Matt. 18:19,20, italics added).

In this passage our Lord taught his followers the right approach to God in the matter of united prayer. Burgess and Lovelace have provided this serviceable outline.

1. *Why united prayer succeeds and is powerful.* It recognizes our common membership in God's family.
2. *When united prayer succeeds,* it demonstrates the principles of united consent: "If two of you shall agree." It shows the presence of the unseen Christ: "I am in the midst."
3. *What united prayer secures.* It deepens our mutual fellowship. It strengthens our personal faith. It in-

creases our love and devotion to the Master. It alters the course of history because history is *His story.*

The Problem of Hindrances

Cowper's expressive prayer-hymn commences with the lines,

> *What various hindrances we meet*
> *In coming to the Mercy Seat!*
> *Yet who, that knows the worth of prayer,*
> *But wishes to be often there?*

Hindrances to prayer are many and manifold, external and internal. Satan, knowing that prayer is the arena of conflict and victory for the believer, uses all of his cunning to destroy the effectiveness of prayer. He knows how to use outward circumstances and interruptions, apathy, straying thoughts, and indolence within for the weakening of the cable heavenward.

There are times when circumstances make it hard to pray. Job found this to be so when he lost his dear ones, his house, his wealth, and his health. "Behold, I cry out of wrong, but I am not heard . . . " Job said (19:7). Jeremiah, when the sorrows of captive Zion were overwhelming his compassionate soul, found it hard to pray (Lam. 3:8,44). His persevering prayers were ultimately victorious, however, and in the prophet's dark hour God was his Light.

Are you sitting in the shadows without much time for prayer and meditation? Are your circumstances "ganging up" on you until it seems as if you lift up your hands into empty space? Is yours this complaint,

Lord, I am tired. I can bring to Thee
Only a heavy weight of tiredness.
I kneel, but all my mind's a vacancy,
And conscious only of its weakness—
Can it be prayer, this dragging dreariness?

No, such dragging dreariness is not conducive to effectual prayer.

Interruptions form another external hindrance to prayer. We retire to pray, but the children cry, the telephone rings, the door bell clangs, salesmen call. The more intent we are on concentrated prayer, the more interruptions there seem to be. As Samuel Zwemer points out, though, we can be patient with such interruptions and make them stepping stones instead of stumbling blocks in the way of prayer if we will only study the example of Jesus. How wonderful He was at making every interruption an opportunity for the exercise of His healing power or His comforting words (Mark 6:34,56)!

Forced to relinquish our posture in prayer, we can remain in the spirit of prayer and as we go to the phone or the door, pray for those who have unknowingly interrupted our blessed moments of communion with God. "If you are interrupted, let the interruption be not an irritation, but an interpretation. . . . The season of prayer will be richer for the mastery of interruption. . . . Evangelize the inevitable."

Other hindrances making true prayer difficult or impossible are indolence, pride, selfishness, formality, idols of the heart, jealousy, and ruptured relationships. The Book of Daniel makes it clear that there are determined, satanic hindrances to prayer. All obstacles, however, are not long in vanishing if we have more purpose in prayer and learn how to pray in the Spirit.

The Problem of Delayed Answers

Some prayers appear to pass unanswered. But their answers are not denied—only delayed. We are apt to misjudge the seemingly slow movements of God. In our rash haste we want immediate answers. We have to learn as Mary and Martha did, that His delays are not denials (John 11:6). The mills of God may appear to grind slowly but they grind exceedingly well. It has been said that "when our prayers make long voyages, they come back laden with richer cargoes of blessings"; and "when God keeps us waiting for an answer, He gives liberal interest for the interval."

The parable of the unjust judge teaches us to persevere in prayer (Luke 18:1–14). There may be delays seeming to indicate that God does not care. Jesus was silent when faced by the Canaanite woman. "He answered her not a word." But to the chagrin of the disciples, the needy woman continued her intercession until she got what she wanted (Matt. 15:21–28).

Delayed answers to our prayers are also profitable in that they cause us to search our hearts to make sure that the cause of divine silence is not within ourselves. Monica's prayers for the salvation of her much-loved son, Augustine, were delayed but not denied. Ultimately, God answered that mother's cries, and her gifted son was saved and became one of the choice saints of the church. "Blessed are all they that wait for Him" (Is. 30:18). Often delays are for our greater benefit. We are not always ready to receive the gifts we seek. "We want to pluck our mercies green, but God waits until they are ripe."

It may seem as a triumph of faith when answers come swiftly on the heels of our prayers, but delays make for discipline. Feverish faith is weak and must be taught to wait. Often we intercede for unbelieving relatives, yet no answer comes. We come to realize that we must wrestle like Jacob, pant like David, hope like Elijah, persist like Bartimaeus, and weep like Jeremiah and Jesus before answers appear.

Moses prayed to go over into Canaan, but his request to enter the Promised Land seemed to be denied (Deut. 3:23–29). He died at Pisgah, and Israel entered Canaan without their leader. Yet some fifteen hundred years later, the prayer of Moses was answered. Then we find him on the mount of the Transfiguration.

Elijah was mighty in prayer, and God answered all his prayers except one. Under the juniper tree, suffering from mental and physical exhaustion, the prophet prayed that he might die. Mercifully, God did not take him at his word. The prayers of a despondent, fretful, overtired saint are seldom valid. Later, Elijah went to heaven in a more glorious way than that of death.

David wanted to build the house of God. His heart was set on such a task, and he prayed much about it. God praised him for wanting to do so but forbade his execution of the task. His prayers were answered in Solomon's day.

If your sincere prayer appears to pass unanswered, you must not be weary in well-doing. All Spirit-inspired prayers are answered in God's good time.

The Problem of Different Answers

If our prayers are not answered in *kind,* they are answered in *kindness.* With his infinite wisdom, God knows that which is best for His children and answers their petitions according to His own intelligence.

The ambitious request of James and John was answered in a way they did not expect. Because they were cousins of our Lord, and members of the inner circle, they thought a favor was due them. They learned that suffering for Christ is the prelude to reigning with Him (Mark 10:35–40; see also Rom. 8:17 and 2 Tim. 2:12). James was the first apostle to suffer martyrdom, and John the last.

Paul prayed for the removal of his thorn. Fervently, he presented his petition three times, and God answered not by removing the burden—but by granting Paul sufficient grace to carry it. This thorn, the messenger of Satan sent to buffet the apostle, became the minister of God to bless him, enabling Paul "to glory in his infirmities that the power of Christ might rest upon him." God gave His servant a larger answer to his prayer. Paul's experience teaches us to be patient with unanswered prayer and to be thankful when an unanticipated answer comes.

The most agonized petition Jesus ever made was not immediately granted. "Father," he cried in the garden, "all things are possible unto thee; take this cup away from me: nevertheless not as I will, but as thou wilt." The cup was not taken away. Jesus was not "saved from death" (Heb. 5:7). An angel strengthened Him to drink the bitter cup of suffering (Luke 22:43). Out He went to endure the cross and despise its shame (Heb. 12:2) so that no Christian should ever feel abandoned by his Lord.

The Problem of Unanswered Prayer

The problem of unanswered prayer is acute. We all feel it. Its mystery shrouds our faith at some time or another. We pray to God, but the heavens seem as brass. Distress or rebellion become ours. Can God be indifferent? Has He forgotten us or ceased to care? Our hearts protest with the psalmist: "How long wilt Thou forget me, O LORD? for ever? how long wilt thou hide thy face from me?" (Ps. 13:1). Silence seems to reign, and we are perplexed.

Let us introduce this vexing problem by stating that there are prayers God *must* answer. Because the Christian is in a covenant of union and communion with God, God is bound to honor His commitments. Being redeemed, the pray-er exercises the covenant privilege of prayer. The basis of his bold approach is the blood of the Redeemer (Heb. 4:16 and 10:19,22).

Among the prayers which God must answer are these:

- Prayers for deliverance from sin. "Him that cometh to me I will in no wise cast out" (John 6:37).
- Prayers for holiness of life. "This is the will of God, even your sanctification..." (1 Thess. 4:3).
- Prayers for the infilling of the Spirit. "...how much more shall your heavenly Father give the Holy Spirit..." (Luke 11:13).
- Prayers for relief from physical and material needs, if such is His will. "Call upon me in the day of trouble: I will deliver thee..." (Ps. 50:15).
- Prayers for the Second Advent. "Even so, come, Lord Jesus" (Rev. 22:20).

But the essence of prayer is found in a right relationship with God. If such a relationship is lacking, He is under no obligation to answer prayer.

As we have already seen, there are laws and conditions attached to prayer. Unrestricted promises are hedged about with limitations. Unlimited invitations are surrounded with conditions we sometimes fail to observe. We are commanded to pray for all men, yet there are those for whom we are forbidden to intercede (Jer. 7:16 and 1 John 5:15,16). We ask and receive not, since the ear of God is closed to the petitioner (Lam. 3:44). Because "prayer is the naked intent stretching out to God, our prayers must be clean as well as our hearts."

Among prayers which God cannot answer are these:

- Prayers lacking sincerity and faith (Matt. 6:5,7, Heb. 11:6 and James 1:6,7).
- Prayers said to avoid taking action (Ex. 14:15 and Josh. 7:7–13).
- Prayers inspired by carnal motives (James 4:2,3).
- Prayers framed to change God's decrees (Deut. 3:23–27).
- Prayers disregarding the revealed will of God (1 Sam. 8:9–19).
- Prayers arising from an unclean heart (Ps. 66:18 and Lam. 3:40–44).
- Prayers desirous of averting necessary chastisement (2 Sam. 12:16–18 and 2 Cor. 12:7–9).
- Prayers seeking the recall of lost opportunities (Luke 13:25–28).
- Prayers accompanied by unconfessed sin (1 John 1:8–10).
- Prayers fashioned out of meaningless and repetitious phrases (Matt. 6:7).
- Prayers offered in foolish pride and arrogance (Prov. 8:13).
- Prayers prompted by selfish motives (James 4:2,3). (Little Tommy went to stay with his aunt, who asked him, "I hope, Tommy, I *do* hope you say your prayers *every*

night?'' "Not every night, Auntie. You see, some nights I don't want anything.")

- Prayers arising out of a heart full of ill will and hatred toward others (Matt. 5:24).

The following lines by Annie Lind Woodworth are full of appeal.

> *Unanswered, does your prayer remain*
> *Though oft with tears you plead?*
> *And watch and wait and wonder if*
> *God does not care or heed?*
>
> *Unanswered? Well, perhaps, dear heart,*
> *You may have asked amiss;*
> *Is it God's glory that you seek,*
> *Or selfish avarice?*
>
> *How often selfish motives form*
> *A prayer God cannot grant;*
> *None can deceive th' Omniscient One*
> *With merely pious cant.*
>
> *Oh, that we might all clearly see*
> *That God will not be mocked;*
> *Against impostors, the door*
> *Of answered prayer is locked.*
>
> *Deep in some recess of your heart,*
> *Perhaps some stubborn sin*
> *Forbids the righteous God to grant*
> *The answer you would win.*
>
> *Perchance an Achan, in the camp,*
> *Bars answer to your prayer;*
> *When he receive confessing grace,*
> *Your answer will be there.*
>
> *Upon the hindrances God throws*
> *His searchlight, powerful, strong;*

But how we squirm, and fain would think
We misconstrue the wrong.

Unanswered? Tested one, pray on—
God will allay each fear—
Give grace and courage to endure
Till answers shall appear.

A little more of suffering,
Of pain and tears for thee;
A little more of trustful prayers,
Then—answers thou shalt see.

Unanswered? No! For even now
God's hand is working out
A plan by which, eventually,
That hindrance He will rout.

Often we receive not because we ask amiss. Ignorance as to God's requirements and the principles of prayer prevents the answer. This is why the specific ministry of the Spirit has been provided. In our prayer infirmity, He is the divine Helper (Rom. 8:26,27).

It remains to be said that while God does answer some of the prayers of the unconverted, He has not promised to do so. All promises of answered prayer are given to the regenerated children—to those in covenant relationship with Him as their heavenly Father.

Are you facing the problem of unanswered prayer? You are grieved because, as far as you know, your heart is right in God's sight, your motives are pure, and your requests are legitimate enough—yet no answer comes. Do not cease to pray. Sometimes, God is silent in His love (Zeph. 3:17). Because of His inscrutable wisdom, He knows what is best for you. He has answers beyond your expected answers. When all the mysteries of life are unraveled, then you will praise Him for your unanswered prayers and "bless the Hand that guided and the Heart that planned."

When fuller, perfect light is ours, we will understand that "No" was an answer, as well as "Yes." Often we hear it said, "God didn't answer my prayer." But He did. He may not have given what was insisted upon, any more than we would give a child a serpent that looked like a fish because he begged for it, or a stone shaped like a piece of bread (Luke 11:11). Yet He does answer in His own way, which is ever the best way. What we deem to be refusals are the only answers possible to His love, wisdom, and truth.

Many prayers, unanswered while a person still lives, are fully answered after death. These are "golden vials, full of odors, which are the prayers of the saints" (Rev. 5:8; see also 8:3), constantly remembered by God.

Mr. Badman's wife was deeply concerned over the lost state of her husband, but John Bunyan made her say: "Are my prayers lost? Are they forgotten? Are they thrown over the bar? No! They are hanged upon the horns of the Golden Altar, and I must have the benefit of them myself, that moment that I shall enter the gate at which the righteous nation that keepeth truth shall enter. My prayers are not lost. My tears are yet in God's bottle."

Yes, at daybreak our hearts will confess:

> *He answered prayer—not in the way I sought,*
> *Nor in the way that I had thought he ought;*
> *But in His own good way, and I could see*
> *He answered in the fashion best for me.*

14

The Inspirer of Prayer

Each Person of the blessed Trinity is related to the exercise of prayer. We have access to the Father, through the Son, by the Spirit (Eph. 2:18). To be specific,

1. God the Father hears and answers prayer (Ps. 17:6, Matt. 7:11, and Heb. 11:6). Graciously, He permits us to approach Him at all times.
2. God the Son presents our imperfect prayers and blends them with His perfect propitiation (Heb. 7). He is our Ladder, set up on earth, by which we ascend to God. He bridges both worlds. All prayers must be in His name (John 14:13,14).
3. God the Spirit is the inspirer of true prayer (Rom. 8:26,27). How dependent we are upon the Spirit as we come to pray! Often we are inclined to ask what would be harmful to us if granted. As Shakespeare said, "We ignorant of ourselves, beg often our own harm." Not knowing how to pray correctly, the Spirit is at hand to prompt our prayers and purify our motives (James 4:3).

The Scriptures teach that the Holy Spirit is "the Spirit of...supplications" (Zech. 12:10) and therefore is the

Source and Sphere of our prayers (Rom. 8:14–27, Gal. 4:6,7, Eph. 6:18, and Jude 20). We read, "He cries," and "we cry," suggesting, as Andrew Murray says, "a wonderful blending of the divine and human cooperation in prayer."

When the Holy Spirit takes possession of the soul and becomes essentially the Spirit of intercession, and as such overcomes our inability to pray properly, He is our aid in prayer. He covers every prayer of the mind and heart, whether in the nature of supplication, confession, intercession, praise, or adoration. Without the Holy Spirit, our prayers are as lifeless as a body without a soul, as ineffective as an arrow without a bow.

"The Spirit," as Norman Harrison states it, "is at once the guide of prayer and the guarantor of its success." Let us try to analyze the outstanding features of this deep truth.

The Spirit Is the Inspirer of Prayer

The divine Spirit first brings the soul into right relationship with God, and the right and privilege of the children of God to pray becomes theirs (Gal. 4:6,7). The desire and ability to pray are made possible by the Spirit. Sonship is the true starting point of all access to God. Fear, with its enslaving influence, is driven out, and the spirit of adoption takes its place. The Spirit becomes the filial Spirit, whereby we cry, "Abba, Father!"

Spirit-inspired prayer is impossible without an *act of memory,* by which our sins and divine mercy are recalled. It is the function of the Spirit to bring all things to our remembrance.

There must be also an *act of the mind.* The Spirit enables us to choose our words and express ourselves in fitting language. He can deliver from distraction and grant us definite concentration. The Spirit quickens the mind and the emotions. He prepares, possesses, and prompts the mind, so that we can continue in prayer. The difference between saying prayers and *praying* is having a Spirit-possessed mind. He teaches us to pray, not by outward forms, but by inward compulsion. As the Spirit of wisdom, He prevents us from uttering unwise petitions.

We must likewise know something of *the act of love*, which enables us to be concerned sympathetically with the needs of others. As the Spirit of love, He sheds abroad the love of God in our hearts (Rom. 5:5).

The Spirit Arouses the Soul

God's gracious Spirit opens to the child of God a vision of a new world of purity and power by revealing the contrast between the old, natural life and the new spiritual life in Christ.

Once within, the Spirit awakens desires for communion with God, to whom we had been strangers. Through His illuminating grace and promptings, we are made conscious of our needs and how to pray about them. What we do not know, the Spirit knows! Thus it is He who works in our hearts, begetting earnest longings for those things which please God. Prayer will never enable us to attain deeper holiness of life unless it is prayer in the Spirit.

Paul's exhortation about praying in the Spirit goes down to the depths and includes more than an ordinary, coherent experience or expression in prayer. It refers to those unfathomed depths in man where there are feelings and yearnings so mysterious that our minds cannot give them definite form or correct articulation. In this obscure realm, deep in human personality where our yearnings originate, the Spirit moves with perfect familiarity and sympathizes with these mysterious longings for which the only language is a sigh or a cry. "He that searcheth the hearts knoweth what is the mind of the Spirit..." (Rom. 8:27).

If we were all we should be and could pray correctly, there would be no need for the Spirit's help. But being imperfect and beset with weakness and ignorance, the prayer ministry of the Spirit is constantly necessary.

The Spirit Intercedes for Us

Christians are blessed with two divine intercessors: One in heaven, the Other in the heart. Paul explains how the Spirit acts as our Intercessor (Rom. 8:26,27). The Lord Jesus Christ is in heaven, ever interceding for us (Heb. 7:25); He is our Advocate on high (Heb. 9:24 and 1 John 2:1). The Spirit is within, prompting our prayer; Christ is above, presenting our petition. The Spirit is "the chamber advocate," preparing our case; Christ is "the court advocate," presenting our case. Thus, as James Montgomery puts it, we have a twofold plea: "Hear me, for Thy Spirit pleads; hear, for Jesus intercedes."

The Spirit prays *in*, as well as *with*, and *for* us. In some profound manner His personality is identified with ours for the purpose of intercession. As God's free Spirit, He joins with our spirit and thus makes our prayers His own, or, rather, creates them within our minds. As the Spirit of intercession, He intercedes within us, just as Christ exercises His intercessory work in heaven (Rom. 8:34). The Spirit lays bare all the deep and hidden needs of the saints;

Christ, in merit of His death and resurrection, pleads for the meeting of such needs.

> *No prayer is made on earth alone*
> *The Holy Spirit pleads;*
> *And Jesus, on the eternal Throne,*
> *For sinners intercedes.*

Two features in connection with the groaning of the Spirit must be observed: These unutterable groanings are known and understood by God, and they are in accordance with the will of God, which is the keynote of all true intercession.

The Spirit Bestows Full Assurance of Faith

What we seek in prayer, believing, we receive. Inspiring us to pray, the Spirit also produces a corresponding faith so that true prayer becomes the prayer of faith, which enables us to ask believingly (Heb. 10:22). This assurance produces a clear recognition of God as the Source who supplies all our needs (James 1:17). Such assurance also unfolds the power and the willingness of God to bestow His good things through His Son and by His Spirit (Eph. 2:18).

If we would guard ourselves from deadness and despondence in the inner chamber, then we must do as the saintly Andrew Murray suggests.

1. We must firmly believe, as a divine reality, that the Spirit of God's Son, the Holy Spirit, is in us.
2. We must understand all the Spirit desires to accomplish in us. His work in prayer is closely connected with His other work.

3. We must recognize His claim to the full possession of our lives. As the soul has the whole body for its dwelling place and service, so the Holy Spirit must have our body and soul as His dwelling place, entirely under His control. Then, and then only, can He function as the Spirit of prayer!

15

Christt at Prayer

We often refer to the prayer in Matthew 6 as the "Lord's Prayer," but we are not told that Jesus prayed that prayer Himself. Seeing the Master in prayer, the disciples said to Him, "Lord, teach us to pray," and then He gave them that model prayer which is remarkable in its simplicity and scope.

But in John 17 we find a prayer that Jesus Himself prayed. In this high priestly prayer of our Lord, we discover the method of all true prayer, a method all of us ought to adopt in our prayers. So often we miss a great deal in our prayer life simply because we have no method. There ought to be as much method about our praying as there is about our Bible study, preaching, and teaching. We need to learn how to concentrate and to be more specific in our petitions. If we do so, our prayer life will be enriched. If you meditate upon the Lord's high priestly prayer, you will discover that it moves in three distinct circles. This is an example that we should follow.

For instance, in the first eight verses of John 17, the Lord Jesus prays about Himself. The Father and the Son are in sweet communion, and the Son is talking to the Father about His own life and work on earth.

Then in verse 9, there comes a distinct change, and until the end of verse 19, Jesus prays for His own. "I pray for them: I pray not for the world"—is how this section commences.

At verse 20, the third circle is reached. From this verse to the end of the chapter, the Lord prays for men and women in general. "Neither pray I for these alone [His disciples round about Him], but for them also which shall believe on me through their word." He saw the vista of the ages and thought of all those who were to listen to the blessed word, and who, through receiving the Lord Jesus Christ, would become part of His body.

So the Lord prayed first for Himself, next for the church, and finally for the world. The first part was personal, the second part was particular, and the third part was general.

As we examine the prayer more closely, we see that Jesus uses the term *Father* in a threefold way. For example, in the first section, when the Lord is communing with the Father about His own work, He uses the single filial term *Father* twice. First, in verse 1, "These words spake Jesus, and lifted up His eyes to heaven, and said, Father, the hour is come; glorify thy Son, that the Son also may glorify thee." And in verse 5, "Now, O Father, glorify thou me with thine own self with the glory which I had with thee before the world was." Here we see the Father and the Son together, and such communion constitutes the holy of holies.

Then as the second part of the prayer begins in verse 11, Jesus addresses God in a very unique way. He refers to Him as "Holy Father." This is the only time God is mentioned in this way in the Bible. As this section of our Lord's prayer is studied, it becomes apparent that the thrust of the petition is that the Lord's own might be sanctified. "Sanctify them through thy truth: thy word is truth" (v. 17). So because He

118

desires His own to be holy, Jesus addresses God in this way, "Holy Father," as if to say, "Because thou art holy, I desire my own to reveal thy holiness." "Be ye holy, even as I am holy," and because of the holiness of God, it is imperative for us to allow the indwelling Holy Spirit to transform us too into holy people.

In the last section of the prayer, beginning with verse 25, Jesus addresses God with the words, "O righteous Father." In this closing section our Lord has before Him the multitudes of the dawning church age who would be brought under the sway of His gospel. He addresses God thus, "O righteous Father," because the basis of our gospel appeal is the righteousness of God. We know that men and women can be saved and made part of the mystic fabric we know as the church because the righteousness of God has been revealed in the finished work of Jesus. Because of His righteousness, sinners can be freely forgiven and cleansed on the basis of the finished work of the Cross.

Christ Prays for Himself

Now let us return to the first part of our Lord's prayer, namely verses 1–8 where the Lord is found praying for Himself. Looking carefully at these words you will find that Jesus tells the Father four things about Himself, and all of those statements commence in the same way. There are four "I haves." The first are in verse 4, "I have glorified thee on the earth: I have finished the work which thou gavest me to do." Verse 6, "I have manifested thy name unto the men which thou gavest me out of the world...." Verse 8, "I have given unto them the words which thou gavest me..." A word on each of these will be beneficial.

"I have glorified thee on the earth." What a confession

to make! And our Lord could make it, for in all of His works and words and ways, He glorified the Father. He had ever sought to bring glory to God, so He asks in this prayer that He might also have the glory which He had shared with the Father from the beginning. I am sure this is one thing that greatly impresses our mind as we read the gospel story. At His incarnation, our Lord in respect to His humanity died to self in that He became subordinate to the Father and dependent upon the Holy Spirit. And because of His subordination to the Father's will, you find Him seeking the glory of God.

I pray that all of us may come to the end of our days saying to the Lord Jesus, "I have glorified thee on the earth." But do we live for the glory of God? Sadly, it is possible to be eaten up with self-glory. "For a man to search out his own glory," said Solomon, "is no glory at all," and nothing can mar our service for the Master like self-glory.

The story is told of a minister who tried in every possible way to honor God. He was gifted and confronted the temptation in his own heart for self-glory by training himself to say, as he stood before a congregation to preach, "Now, my soul, honor bright, is this for the glory of God?" More of us should find a similar method to subdue our natural urge to glorify self.

In the Scottish Catechism we read, "Man's chief end is to glorify God and to enjoy Him forever." It is said that a minister, who went around to the homes of his church to catechize the members and their children, came one day into a home to catechize a boy. He asked, "My lad, what is man's chief end?"

"Man's chief end," the boy replied, "is to glorify God and to enjoy Him forever."

"Quite right," said the minister.

Then, very timidly, the boy said to the minister, "But could you tell me what God's chief end is?"

The minister was non-plussed, but thought for a minute and then said, "I am afraid I cannot answer you."

The lad said, "God's chief end is to glorify man and to enjoy him forever."

If we live for the glory of God in this life, we know from this very prayer that we are to be glorified by God, for the express wish of our praying Savior is that we might be with Him and share His glory. Let us have before us the glory of God, for nothing less can satisfy His heart.

The second thing Jesus told His Father about Himself was, *"I have finished the work which thou gavest me to do."* Our Lord was anticipating the Cross when He prayed this prayer. Later, in His agony, the last cry to escape His lips was, "It is finished." This was not the cry of a victim. Our Lord did not mean that He was glad to come to the end of His own physical anguish. His cry, "It is finished," was the shout of a Victor. We are born to live; Christ was born to die. He came from glory with the express purpose in mind of going to the cross to die for our redemption. So when He uttered that cry, "It is finished," He had in mind the overthrow of Satan and the deliverance of souls from the bondage of sin. These words, then, refer to the finished work of Christ. And by that one act, that supreme sacrifice of His, He spoiled principalities and powers and made it possible for the sons and daughters of Adam's race to be delivered from the penalty of sin.

"I have finished the work which thou gavest me to do." The devil tried to keep Jesus from the cross, for he knew that by that one act, his kingdom would be forever spoiled. The Master, however, set His face steadfastly toward Jerusalem and took the blood-red way until ultimately He died upon the cross for our salvation.

"I have finished the work which thou gavest me to do." I wonder if we will be able to pray thus? Are we striving to complete the task so that when we come to the end of our sojourn here below, we, too, may have grace to pray with the Redeemer, "I have finished the work"? I fear that so many· of us are like the man in the gospel story who began to build but was not able to finish. We are good at fits and starts; our service is spasmodic and intermittent. There is not the same completeness about our ministry that characterized the work of our Lord.

We think of very many in church life and work who seek to serve the Lord in some sphere or the other, but who seem to tire and through various circumstances resign and do not finish their tasks. Maybe you were once very active for the Savior, but you resigned your position for some reason or another. I want you to know that the resignations of discouraged workers are not valid.

On Calton Hill, Edinburgh, there are six or seven massive columns standing above the skyline. Soon after the French Revolution, it was the desire of the city to erect a large Athenian building on the hill. They sent out appeals and tried to gather money. Money flowed in, soon reaching thousands of dollars, but somehow the subscriptions ceased, and the city was able to build only the six or seven columns. There they stand, today being known as "Pride and Poverty." The city began to build but was not able to finish.

One thing that keeps me faithful to my task is this: When the day breaks and the shadows flee away and I find myself in the presence of the Lord, He will show me the original plan He had for my life—the plan for my career and my character. I pray that when I stand before Him, my life and His divine pattern will fully correspond.

"I have manifested thy name unto the men which thou gavest me out of the world." The word *name* represents the character and personality of the person concerned, so in effect our Lord is saying in this phrase, "I have manifested Thy nature or character unto the men Thou gavest Me out of the world."

Jesus Christ was the culmination of the revelation of God. The world needed to know what God was like, so He came and indwelt a human body. The Lord Jesus was God manifested in the flesh. If we want to know what God is like, then we must study the life and teaching of the Lord Jesus. That is why in John 14:9 He says, "He that hath seen me hath seen the Father." He was the personification of the love of the Father. He reflected the attributes of God.

I wonder if we show what the Lord Jesus is like. This is our solemn obligation, not only to glorify the Lord, not only to finish our God-given tasks, but day by day to reveal something of the beauty of the Lord Jesus.

It was easy for men to believe in God after they had seen Christ. I wonder if it is easier for men and women round about us to believe in the Savior after they come in contact with us. We may be very orthodox and yet so un-Christlike. The world is yearning for the practical manifestation of the life of Christ in His followers. Many moderns relegate the Lord Jesus to the level of ordinary humanity. We are told it is enough simply to emulate the example of Jesus. But there is no salvation by the mere example of Christ. It is found only in a willingness to allow Him to dominate every part of our life that through us He might express

Himself. Christ lives in me. It may be that some people round about you may be won for the Lord when they see the likeness of Christ in you.

I remember hearing once at the Keswick Conference the Sadhu, the great Indian Christian. How greatly impressed I was with his demeanor. Tall, stately, and commanding in his long robe, with a beautiful white turban wound about his head, he immediately attracted attention. When he had first arrived in London, he made his way to the home of Walter Sloane, then secretary of the conference. The maid opened the door and when she saw this black man, she turned back somewhat afraid. He gave his name and asked to see Mr. Sloane. She told her master that there was a man to see him. He asked the name, but the maid said she did not know; it was a very strange name.

"Well, what is he like?" asked Mr. Sloane.

"Well, he is like Jesus," she replied.

I wonder if others can say that about us? Oh, may the beauty of the Lord our God be upon us!

"I have given unto them the words which thou gavest me; and they have received them." This is striking, for it says that Jesus did not originate the truth He preached and taught. Dwelling in the presence of the Father, He received from Him that revelation, which in turn He transmitted. Just as Moses climbed the mount and received the commandments from God and in turn brought them down and gave them to the people, so you find the Lord Jesus waiting upon the Father; and receiving from God a divine revelation, He conveyed it to those around Him. This is our solemn obligation as workers in the vineyard of the Lord, not to disseminate our thoughts about the Word of God, but to communicate the Word of God itself to men and women in need.

By the way, I believe there is a great difference between preachers and messengers. A good many years ago I discovered the distinction between the two, and I bless God for the discovery. The curse of the ministry is that we have far too many preachers, but all too few messengers. If a man sets out to be a popular preacher, then there is the temptation to compromise accordingly. To be sure of his position, he must be prepared to preach to please. This kind of preacher tries to keep his position by pleasing the people before him, so he preaches to the gallery. This is why so many ministers are destitute of spiritual power. They only live that they might be known as preachers.

But a messenger is a man who gazes into the face of the eternal and has burned upon his conscience a message he must declare. It does not matter to him what people say or think about his ministry or his proclamation of a God-given message. Jesus was a messenger. He tarried before the Father, drank in the divine word, and then declared it. And He had to pay the price for His faithfulness. Jesus was not crucified for His miracles. He was crucified for His sayings. It was because of His determination to stand before men and declare what God had revealed to Him that they hurried Him to the cross.

So, we have these four confessions in the first part of this prayer of our Lord: "I have glorified thee on the earth"; "I have finished the work which thou gavest me to do"; "I have manifested thy name unto the men which thou gavest me out of the world"; "I have given unto them the words which thou gavest me; and they have received them." Because Jesus could pray thus about Himself, He could pray with power as He came to intercede for His own. Because His prayer was deeply personal, He had added power as He came to pray for His church and then for the world in general. Let us, too, begin with ourselves, for we can never pray for our brothers and sisters in Christ with any measure of success unless we know what it is to have a deep personal prayer life.

In John 17, then, we have the prayer Jesus prayed. And be assured, beloved, He has never ceased to pray for "He ever liveth to make intercession for us" (Heb. 7:25).

How to Use This Book

1. *To the Pastor who wishes to have a more effective prayer program in his church.*

    Place this volume in the hands of all your church officials and Sunday school teachers. Ask them to study the book and then share, individually and as a group, the meaning of this volume for the immediate and long-range prayer development of your church.

    There are great Bible study and sermon suggestions to be found in the book's chapter titles and section headings.

2. *To the Christian Teacher.*

    Organize a prayer school with two teaching periods each night for five nights. Place a copy of this book in the hands of each one in your class. Invite them to read and discuss the volume.

    Use this volume as supplementary material for the teaching of prayer to a Sunday school group.

3. *To the Prayer Group Leader.*

    Place a copy of this book in the hands of each member of your prayer group. Invite each person to read, study, and meditate as he faces the total challenge of "how to pray more effectively." Then ask them to bring the book to the prayer group meetings for discussion and sharing.

4. *To Families.*

Place one or more copies of this book in your home. Short sections or quotations may be used in family prayer. Keep a copy on the table by the bed, read one chapter each night.

5. *To business people and other workers.*

Place a copy of this on your desk or where you work. Pause to read from it, at the beginning of the day, at noon, or during coffee breaks. Underscore sentences, mark pages, and list page references.

Get a supply of these books and start giving them to your friends. Do you know a friend—perhaps a "shut-in"—who would like to have this book? Send him or her one today.

Suggested Readings

Prayer literature has greatly enriched the life of the church. Great libraries have extensive bibliographies on prayer. Hymnologies and liturgies enshrine the prayers of the ages. Money is well spent and brings spiritual dividends when it is invested in books dealing with the prayer life of the believer. Among some of the more helpful books the writer consulted in the preparation of this volume, mention must be made of the following works. (Note: Unfortunately, some of these books are no longer being published. For this reason, as a service to readers, I have divided the list into two categories—"In Print" and "No Longer in Print.")

IN PRINT
Bounds, E. M. *Power Through Prayer.* Chicago: Moody Press, 1979. A revolutionary book on the subject.

Hallesby, O. *Prayer.* Minneapolis: Augsburg House, 1975. A unique volume showing us how prayer can become a holy art. This great work is warmly recommended.

Murray, Andrew. *Prayer Life.* Chicago: Moody Press, n.d. A spiritual classic.

NO LONGER IN PRINT
Burgess and Proudlove. *Watching Unto Prayer.* London: Lutterworth

Press, n.d. These one hundred Bible readings on prayer are among the most suggestive to come our way. Worth its weight in gold!

Evans, William. *Why Pray?* Grand Rapids, Michigan: Wm. Eerdmans Co., n.d. An indispensable handbook for all those who desire to know how to pray correctly.

Harrison, Norman B. *His in a Life of Prayer.* Chicago: Moody Press, n.d. Multitudes of Christians, including the writer, have been richly blessed, not only by this volume, but all other's in the "His Series."

Horner, William Wallace. *Let Us Pray.* Montgomery, Alabama: Paragon Press, n.d. A most timely and challenging presentation of the mystery of prayer.

Laubach, Frank C. *Prayer—the Mightiest Force in the World.* New York: Revell, 1946. A courageous presentation of prayer as a dynamic force among men and nations.

Macartney, Clarence E. *Prayer—At the Golden Altar.* A striking treatise on the power of prayer.

Proctor, William. *The Principles and Practice of Prayer.* London: Oliphants, n.d. This homiletical work, printed over fifty years ago, contains some of the most suggestive outlines on prayer. Every preacher should covet these outlines for study.

Sabiers, Karl. *The Prayer Life.* Los Angeles: Robertson Publishing Co., n.d. This booklet is one of the series in the "Christian Study Course."

Talling, Marshall P. *Communion With God, Extempore Prayer.* New York: Revell, 1902. A most outstanding treatment of the principles and practice of prayer.

Zwemer, Samuel. *Taking Hold of God.*

Readers desiring further material on the subject of prayer should consult the list of books given at the back of Dr. Zwemer's volume, also articles on prayer to be found in all reliable Bible dictionaries.

The writer acknowledges his indebtedness to the numerous magazine articles and booklets that he has gathered and filed through the years, as well as to the chapters in sermonic books that he has perused with much profit.